FURNITURE MAKEOVERS

FURNITURE MAKEOVERS

Simple Techniques for Transforming Furniture with
Paint, Stains, Paper, Stencils, and More

BARB BLAIR

PHOTOGRAPHS BY
J. AARON GREENE

FOREWORD BY HOLLY BECKER

CHRONICLE BOOKS
SAN FRANCISCO

Library of Congress Cataloging-in-Publication Data available.

ISBN 978-1-4521-0415-7

Manufactured in China

Designed by Hillary Caudle

Projects are for recreational purposes, not for commercial purposes.

10 9 8 7 6 5 4 3 2 1

Chronicle Books LLC
680 Second Street
San Francisco, California 94107
www.chroniclebooks.com

CONTENTS

FOREWORD

When I first met Barb Blair in person, it was at my book signing in SoHo at Anthropologie. I'll never forget the moment she introduced herself because it was then that the online friendship we'd shared up until that point came full circle. When she gave me a big, warm hug, I knew that Barb and I shared a kinship, an unspoken vibe that you either have with someone or you don't. We are two Southern women (though I currently reside in Germany) who love life and our families, and who have a genuine passion for what we do. At the time, Barb had bright blue highlights in her hair and I was really impressed by that. I don't know why, really—perhaps because she is an expert in her field and so talented, so the edgy flair was a bit unexpected. Barb's energy is infectious, uncomplicated, and authentic. She's a true original, and this quality flows directly from her heart into her work at Knack Studios.

Knack furniture pieces are the essence of Barb. She approaches her work with the same playful positivity with which she approaches her life, and this makes her stand out in the sea of others who are reimagining furniture. A Knack piece is an art piece, and each one has a unique personality—so much personality that each has its own name! Take a look at Prentice (page 128), Jules (page 138), and Eudora (page 154) and you'll see what I'm talking about. There is a certain magic that Barb brings to anything she touches, and since her creativity is limitless, her ideas are always fresh and filled with character.

This book, in which Barb details her inspirations, process, and ideas, will inspire you to add a certain sparkle to your DIY creations. The book will also motivate you to stretch your creative limits because Barb possesses more than talent for refinishing work, she is also a talented teacher and motivator. This is not a dry how-to book; here, Barb becomes your new best friend, hanging out with you in your garage as you sand and spray paint, laughing at your mistakes and celebrating your triumphs along the way. As a design blogger and stylist, I am always looking for fresh home decor ideas, and *Furniture Makeovers* is chock-full of them. I can't wait to keep a copy on my bookshelf and try one of the inspiring projects myself!

When I see Barb again, I hope the tables are turned and that I am at her book signing. This book is truly unique and gives you a rare special peek into Barb's "knack" for furniture transformation so that you can bring a little of her charm into your home.

Love,

Holly Becker
Founder of Decor8blog and author of *Decorate* and *Decorate Workshop*

indeed, I hav[e]

b[e]autiful ink

DECORATE

INTRODUCTION

My love for paint began in 2000, when my husband and I moved into our current house, a sweet yellow ranch home built in the 1970s. From the second we walked into the house, we were in love with the built-in desks, bookshelves, and moldings.

The only problem was that the kitchen cabinets were very dark and dated. This was a problem that we needed to solve, and since we could not afford to tear out and redo everything—we were a young family with two toddlers and a very limited budget—I decided I was going to use paint to update the cabinets. I remember my husband looking at me, and asking, "Are you *sure*?" (After all, I was a stay-at-home mom with two- and four-year-olds!) But I was sure. I went out and purchased a few gallons of cream paint and a dark glaze by Ralph Lauren and got to work transforming my kitchen cabinets.

There are a lot of cabinets, and I had to learn as I went since this was before the time of design blogs and online tutorials. It took me three weeks of working around nap times and late into the evenings after the kids went to bed, but at the end of those three weeks, my love for paint and its transforming power had me hook, line, and sinker. My cabinets still bear the same finish. I don't have the heart to change them, as they are what led me to discover my passion. It is rewarding to take what seems like an impossible and daunting task, roll up your sleeves, do the hard things, and work it out.

After this first experience, I began to paint other pieces in my house. Then I started picking up forlorn pieces off the side of the road and stalking the Goodwill and Salvation Army for hidden treasures. I started experimenting with paint finishes, colors, and hardware until I developed a system and style that really felt right. I am completely self-taught and I guess you could say I learned through trial and error. Once I started transforming pieces, I was hooked. After a while, people started to take notice of my work and expressed interest in purchasing pieces for their own homes.

It was such a thrill for me to begin to create for others, and share with them my passion for furniture transformation! Over the past few years, my business has grown from kitchen cabinets and painting out of my garage to a studio of my very own—Knack, where I paint and create furniture on a daily basis. I now have pieces of furniture in homes all across America, and as far away as Tokyo! It has been exciting to see Knack grow into a thriving, creative business, and I am grateful to be doing what I love every day.

But I am not the only one with the power of furniture transformation in my hands! You, too, can transform pieces of your very own, and without spending an arm and a leg. The wonderful thing about working with furniture is that it only takes a few key ingredients to create a beautiful design. In this book, I have culled together a power list of all my favorite tools plus step-by-step techniques to help you get started. These are the techniques I use every day in my own work. You'll learn how to strip, sand, stain, paint, stencil—and so much more! The last section of the book features thirty before and after photos, showcasing some of my all-time favorite furniture transformations, with tips to help you replicate the looks. I hope that this book will inspire you to discover a creative passion, see potential in the world around you, roll up your sleeves, and create furniture masterpieces of your very own!

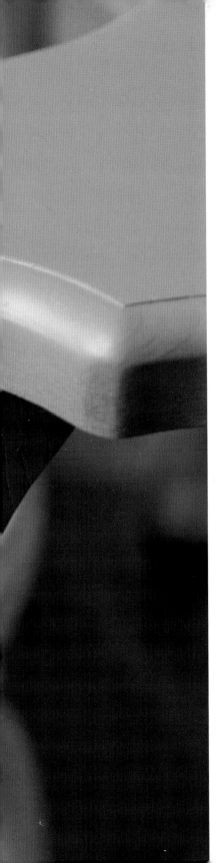

THE HUNT

HOW TO FIND YOUR PERFECT PIECE

WHERE TO LOOK

It is always a great day when it is furniture-hunting day! I love perusing my local hotspots to see what I can find. Some of my favorite places to hunt for furniture are the Salvation Army, Goodwill Clearance stores, estate sales, and local flea markets. Estate sales prove to be the best for me because I can buy in bulk, and the quality of the furniture is usually very high. Even if you are not planning to buy in bulk, estate sales are still a great source for individual furniture pieces. Check your local newspaper for estate sale dates and times. Typically, flea markets and thrift stores are the most inexpensive options for furniture (although I have seen huge price increases over the past two years). When shopping and buying at flea markets, be careful not to get caught up in the moment and forget to really check the piece out well. Sometimes with outdoor flea markets you can miss things like smells, stains, and stability due to the bright sun and uneven ground. Be sure to make an intentional and informed choice based on the recommendations I have listed for you in this chapter. Flea markets can be a fun all-day outing for furniture and many other things, so make sure you bring plenty of cash, tote bags, sunscreen, snacks, and a vehicle large enough to transport all of your finds home! Another way to discover great pieces is to contact some of your local antique dealers. Some antique dealers buy out and host estate sales, and are more than happy to keep you in the loop about their sales. Furniture consignment stores can also be a source of good finds, but in my experience I have found them to be at the higher end in pricing, so I usually do not put them at the top of my list for places to check.

WHAT TO LOOK FOR

PERSONALITY

When buying furniture, I like to spot personality in a piece. I actually give all of my pieces names—like Tilly, Gertrude, Vernon, and Hespa—to bring out their personality a bit. Sometimes the name of a piece is directly related to something that I find interesting about the piece, or relates to the previous owner. I once started work on a piece I bought from an estate sale, only to discover ten poems tucked away behind one of the drawers. I incorporated those poems into the design by permanently lining the little drawer with my favorite ones, and then named the piece after the writer of the poems, "Jenkins." I see each piece as something truly unique and special, and I find great joy in the fact that typically no one sees any value in the pieces that I often get so excited about and can't wait to get started on.

WOOD

First of all, I do not like to work on anything that is not solid wood. I do not even give a second glance to particleboard pieces, or paper veneer pieces. (Paper veneer is a thin wood-grain patterned paper over pressed wood, and it can't be sanded because it has a paper finish.) A wood veneer is fine because it can be sanded, but that is the only veneer that I will consider. I am a solid-wood furniture lover, and believe strongly that any other kind does not lead to the best end result.

CONDITION

The next thing I do after establishing the type of wood is to open the drawer, stick my head in as far as it will go, and take a big sniff. If there is even a hint of smoke, I shut the drawer and walk away. I learned my lesson early on in this area, and have tried everything in the book (and on the Internet) to remove the smell of smoke. It just never leaves. I promise, it is not worth it. The second thing I sniff for is a really strong mold or mildew smell. This is a little bit easier to remove with good bleach and water cleaning, and a few days in the hot sun, but if I had my druthers I would just rather not mess with it either. Since I sell most of my pieces, the furniture must be "smell free" in order for me to move on in my assessment!

Next, I check the drawers. Are all the runners there? Are they wood? Metal? Broken? It is pretty high on most of my clients' lists that the drawers glide smoothly, and so I try to make sure that is the case, or if it is not the case, that it can be fixed relatively easily. I personally shy away from metal drawer runners, as they tend to go along with lesser-quality pieces of furniture. Most pieces that I choose have wooden runners because they hold up much better than metal ones. I also check all of the drawer joints and connecting points to make sure they are secure and not cracked or broken. I love to see a beautiful dovetail joint, where the pieces fit together like a puzzle, and can be easily glued and repaired if needed.

Don't get me wrong, there are times—like when I found this great highboy chest and opened the top drawer only to find that someone had used "L" brackets and a piece of particle board to attach a new drawer back—where I break my own rules because I've fallen in love with a piece and know that it can be fixed. The most important thing is to select a piece that inspires you. But be sure to weigh the cost of the piece against the time and money it will take to repair it before making the final decision. If you are keeping the piece for yourself, you may feel like the cost of the repairs is more than worth it. If you plan to sell it, make sure you can still make a profit!

After you have sniffed out any odors and checked the drawers, check the overall structure of the piece. Is the piece solid, or does it shimmy back and forth when you push on it? If it does shimmy, this is a pretty costly and time-consuming repair, as the piece should probably be completely taken apart and re-glued, so I would move on. If the piece has spindle legs or any kind of leg at all, be sure to check for stability there as well. Ideally, the legs will be solid, unmovable, and free of fractures. Check to see if the legs have been previously cracked or repaired. Was the repair done properly? If so, the structure should be fine. Be careful when lifting and moving pieces, and be sure to remove all the weight off the legs when moving. Do not drag a piece of furniture across the floor, as this will usually end up damaging the legs of the piece. Get help, lift the piece completely off the floor, and move it to the desired location.

SURFACE

Last but not least, examine the overall surface. Is it scratched, is the veneer falling off, are there chips and dings? When painting furniture, a lot of these issues can be glued and wood filled, and once painted you will never know they were there. But it is good to know what you're up against from the beginning. I tend to select pieces that have a limited amount of extensive prep work, so that I can begin working on them right away. But, I have been known to take on some pretty banged-up pieces as well. Just remember that you'll need to give the piece some extra TLC before starting on the fun part.

This is a simple checklist that I go through in my search for furniture pieces, but as with all rules, there will be exceptions. (And believe me, there have been times when my excitement has gotten the better of me, and I have picked a doozy beyond saving.) Evaluate each piece based on the time and energy that you want to put into it, and how much you really love it! The main thing is to look for quality, well-built pieces that will last and can be enjoyed for years to come.

TOOLS & MATERIALS

I've heard that having the right tools makes all the difference when completing a task, and I think there is great truth in that saying. There is nothing like getting halfway through a project and realizing that you do not have the proper tool to complete what you are working on. Here is a list of my favorite tools and materials to help you stock your toolbox, and take some of the guesswork out of furniture refinishing. I also include specific tool lists for each technique as we go along in the book. All of the tools listed here are readily available at your local hardware and craft stores, and are not hard to find. Be sure to have on hand what you need before starting your project!

PAINTS & FINISHES

A

B

C

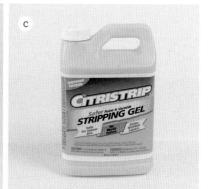

D

E

F

G

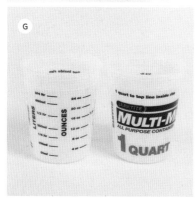

H

AFTER WASH

FIG. A

Made by Klean-Strip, this is a product used for cleaning and preparing a surface after stripping. It removes any leftover residue from the stripping process, but it will not raise the grain of the wood or damage the joints in any way. I always use this product after stripping a piece of furniture to ensure the smoothest and most even finish. The best way to apply After Wash is with a rag. Applying with a rag allows you to wipe down the surface thoroughly without over-saturating. Be sure to wear chemical-resistant gloves when applying After Wash.

CHALK PAINT

FIG. B

The beauty of this product is that it does not require priming or sanding. Chalk Paint can go over old waxes and varnishes, will stick to anything, and is water based. This is an eco-friendly paint that only requires water clean up. It is sold in limited basic colors, but you can combine colors to create as many different shades as you like. This paint is great for both beginning DIY enthusiasts and seasoned veterans who want to have some fun. I love to use polyurethane over this paint instead of using a wax finish. Using polyurethane makes it a little less dull.

CITRISTRIP

FIG. C

This is a natural, biodegradable stripping agent. Just because it is mild smelling and gentle on the eyes and lungs, do not underestimate its power. This product can knock out any stripping project! I use Citristrip whenever I need to remove layers of paint or old varnish from a piece of furniture before applying a new finish. This is the only stripping product I will use in my work, and I highly recommend it over chemical-based strippers.

DANISH OIL

FIG. D

Danish oil is a unique blend of oil and varnish that penetrates deep into wood and hardens in order to protect and enhance the natural beauty of the wood. When I decide to leave legs or bases of furniture pieces unpainted, I like to give them a very light sanding followed by an application of Danish oil.

GLOVES

FIG. E

Always wear plastic gloves when applying chemicals like strippers and stains in order to keep the product from absorbing into your system or damaging your skin. When working with chemicals, you will want to make sure you buy chemical-resistant gloves.

I also have a stash of latex disposable gloves to keep my hands clean while applying stains and nonchemical processes.

LATEX PAINT

FIG. F

Latex is a water-based paint that provides great coverage, is fast drying, and widely available. All latex paint brands are not created equal, however, and you do get what you pay for. I choose paint brands like Benjamin Moore and Ralph Lauren that have high pigmentation and a creamy smooth consistency. Latex paints are easy to clean up with soap and water.

MEASURING CUP

FIG. G

I use a liquid measuring cup to measure milk-paint powders and water formulations when mixing paints. It comes in handy for mixing latex paint formulations too, so that you can keep track of specific color formulations and easily replicate your favorites later on.

MILK PAINT

FIG. H

One of my favorite paints to work with, milk paint gives a truly authentic finish. When I say authentic, I mean that this

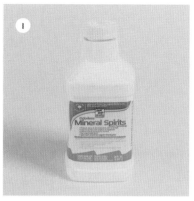

finish looks like it has happened naturally over time. It gives a layered and peeled look that you can't get with any other paint. However, milk paint is finicky, and tends to self-distress in an intense way, so I do not recommend it if you are going for a light distressed or solid look. Milk paint comes in both powder form and premixed cans. I always choose the powder form because I enjoy mixing it together and creating my own consistency. The mixing is not complicated, as it is equal parts water and milk-paint powder. It is a truly "green" paint that is VOC free and leaves no odor when dry. Milk paint is available in twenty classic colors, but you can mix your own colors as well to create custom tints.

ODORLESS MINERAL SPIRITS
FIG. I

Mineral spirits are a general-purpose thinner for oil-based stains and finishes. I personally use mineral spirits not as a thinner, but to clean my tools after the use of an oil-based product. I use the Klean-Strip brand

because it is "green," has no hazardous air pollutants, and is nontoxic and nonflammable. Be sure to follow all safety precautions when using and applying mineral spirits.

PAINT TRAYS
FIG. J

You'll need trays to contain the paint for your projects. It is important that your trays are kept very clean. I use mostly latex paints, so cleaning the trays with soap and warm water immediately after the project is effective in keeping them free of flaking paint. However, if you find that you don't tend to rinse right away, or if you are using something other than water-based products, I suggest buying disposable plastic liners for these trays to make cleanup fast and easy and extend the life of your paint tray. You do not want particles of leftover paint from previous furniture projects interfering with the finish on your current piece. For those of you worried about the environmental friendliness of plastic disposable trays, you can now purchase biodegradable

trays made from 100 percent recycled material at your local Home Depot.

PAINTBRUSHES
FIG. K

Besides my hands, paintbrushes are the most important tools in my work. You will need small flat brushes for those hard-to-reach places, tiny brushes for detail work, and sash brushes for the larger surfaces. Here are my personal favorites:

▶ **China Brush:** Sometimes these are also called white bristle brushes, and I use only the Purdy White China Brush series in my work. This is the brush to use when applying all clear-coat polyurethanes and stains. Inexpensive synthetic-bristle brushes will leave obvious brush strokes in your finish.

▶ **Detail Brushes:** I picked up a mega paintbrush pack at the craft store a few years ago that had paintbrushes in all different sizes. These brushes prove invaluable for painting tiny details, edges, and trim.

L

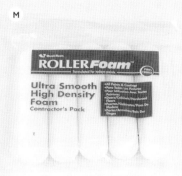

M

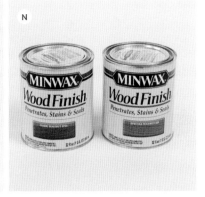

N

▶ **Sash Brush:** My favorite paintbrush to use with latex paints is the Nylox series made by Purdy. I always get great results with this brush and am never disappointed. I use this paintbrush for the majority of my painting projects. It is the perfect soft brush for all latex paints.

▶ **Wax Brush:** This brush is essential for applying wax, because it is round, soft, and gets into all of the detailed areas while providing smooth, even coverage for the entire surface.

POLYURETHANE
FIG. L

Polyurethane is a clear, fast-drying finish used to protect both the porous wood and the painted surfaces in all of your furniture projects. I prefer to use a satin finish; it adds just the right amount of shine to give a piece a professional finished look. I typically do not use glossy polyurethane finishes, as I prefer a more muted shine. I use both water-based and oil-based polyurethane for the projects in this book. I highly recommend an oil-based polyurethane finish for long-lasting results on high-traffic surfaces. The product that I recommend for this is the Arm-R-seal Oil & Urethane Topcoat in satin finish by General Finishes. I recommend applying oil-based products with a rag or China brush. If you want a super-smooth finish using oil-based products, I recommend using a sprayer.

ROLLERS
FIG. M

Foam rollers are used to create that ultra-smooth finish on furniture and cabinets, and work great with latex and water-based finishes. Rollers do not work that well with oils and stains because air can become trapped, leaving bubbles in the finish. (This is called orange peeling.)

SHOP TOWELS

Shop towels are the hardest working paper towels out there, and are much thicker and more durable than regular paper towels. You can buy them in rolls or by the box. They are lint free, and perfect for not only cleaning up messes but for applying stains. Shop towels are completely disposable (just make sure to dispose of them properly if you have used them to apply chemicals). I use disposable towels over lint-free cloth rags because I have found that even though cloth rags claim to be lint free, they still tend to leave lint on the surface of the furniture.

STAINS
FIG. N

The only stains I use on my furniture projects are Minwax Special Walnut and Dark Walnut stains. Minwax stain is a wood finishing stain that seals, penetrates, and protects with built-in polyurethane. I use it to protect and finish my pieces, but also to add depth and age through application over paint. Stain stands alone as a finish since it has built-in sealers, so you will not need to add any other finish over the stain once it is applied.

GLUES & BINDINGS

BONDO ALL-PURPOSE PUTTY

FIG. A

Putty is ideal for large wood repairs. I use Bondo putty mainly for large veneer repairs. Bondo is a two-part process, mixing a polyester resin and a hardener together to make putty. (Everything you need comes together, so just follow the mixing and application instructions included with the product for the best results.) Apply the putty with a putty spatula to the area needing repair. Make sure you smooth down the surface as much as possible to limit the amount of sanding you have to do. Once the putty hardens completely, you can sand and shape it as needed. Bondo requires a bit more detailed mixing and applying compared to wood filler, but I recommend it for larger repairs, as wood filler can crack.

DOUBLE-SIDED MOUNTING TAPE

FIG. B

Double-sided mounting tape is strong, durable, and perfect for holding down paper liners inside furniture drawers. I like to use double-sided tape versus permanently adhering, so that the paper can be easily changed out later on. This tape is tough and super strong, but can be removed by simply pulling up the paper and peeling the tape away from the surface.

FIDDES WAX

FIG. C

This is my favorite wax to use on furniture projects. I use wax mostly on milk paint and Chalk Paint finishes, but I do use it over latex paint finishes as well. Wax has a different level of shine than stains and polyurethanes.

It starts out cloudy but buffs to a beautiful natural shine. It is creamy, easy to manipulate, quick drying, and toluene-free. There is little to no odor with this wax, and with the quick drying time, you can begin to buff in as little as three minutes. I use the light clear wax when I do not want to alter the color of the painted finish but want to add a beautiful matte shine, and the rugger brown shade when I want to add both an aged depth and a matte shine to the finish.

FROGTAPE

FIG. D

FrogTape comes in green and yellow—the yellow for pre-painted surfaces and the green for unpainted surfaces. It is an easily removable tape used to create straight lines in painting. I use FrogTape to mask off all

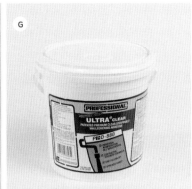
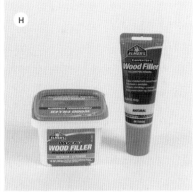

the edges when painting a piece of furniture. I believe in having clean, perfectly straight lines. There is no room for sloppy overbrushing when creating a new piece.

GORILLA GLUE

FIG. E

Gorilla Glue is 100 percent waterproof, and is sandable, paintable, and stainable. It differs from wood glue in that it expands as it dries, creating a hardened "foam" form, whereas wood glue does not expand at all as it dries. It is ideal for all tough furniture repairs, including structural and weight-bearing repairs. A little goes a long way with this particular glue because of the expansion, so make sure to use it sparingly! Also, be sure to clamp your piece appropriately as you glue to keep everything in place.

MOD PODGE

FIG. F

This is an all-in-one glue, sealer, and finish. I use this product specifically with paper and découpage projects. It is totally nontoxic, with easy soap and water cleanup. Mod Podge is available in several decorative finishes, but I use the matte finish in all of my cut and paste projects because I apply polyurethane over the Mod Podge for the final finish.

WALLPAPER PASTE

FIG. G

Wallpaper paste can be used with both prepasted and nonpasted wallpaper applications. However, each wallpaper company is different in how they want their wallpaper applied, so be sure to read the application instructions before you apply. Some require you to apply paste directly to the wallpaper, and some require you to apply it directly to the surface to be papered. I use a water-based, clear, nonstaining, soap and water cleanup paste for all of my wallpaper applications on furniture. I've found that the water-based formula works expertly with specialty, hand-printed, and delicate papers.

WOOD FILLER

FIG. H

I use wood filler to repair small holes, scratches, and gouges. Apply the filler with a putty spatula, and be sure to wipe your spatula clean when the project is complete. (If you let the wood filler build up on your putty spatula, it will start to hinder the smoothness of your fills.) Wood filler is easily painted, sanded, stained, and you can clean it up with just soap and water.

WOOD GLUE

FIG. E

Wood glue is ideal for both small and large wood furniture repairs, on both indoor and outdoor furniture. If the repair is structural or weight bearing, it is imperative that you apply the proper clamping and pressure while gluing to ensure a complete repair. If the pieces you are gluing are not perfectly aligned, the durability of the piece will be compromised. It is important that you leave the clamps in place for the full drying time. Wood glue is paintable, sandable, and stainable.

CUTTING & SANDING

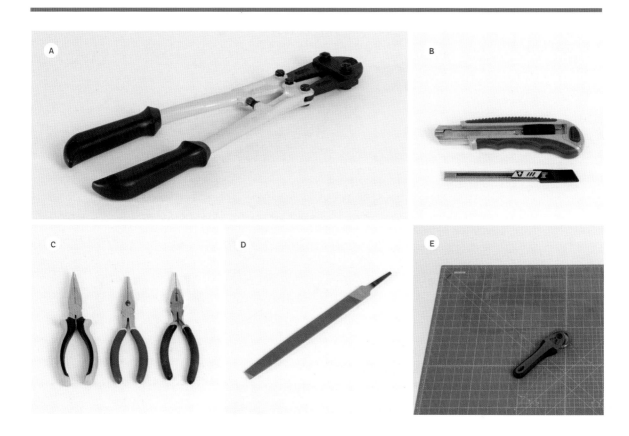

BOLT CUTTERS
FIG. A

This tool is heavy duty—and a little intimidating—but awesome for cutting through heavy, dense materials, like those pesky long screws that come standard on knobs and cabinet hardware. Some people do not like the long screw sticking out inside the drawer, so use the bolt cutters to trim that screw down. When trying to remove old hardware or an unwanted screw or bolt that will just not give, reach for the bolt cutters and your job is done.

CRAFT KNIVES
FIG. B

Similar to X-ACTO knives, I choose to use craft knives for the easily retractable blades and the ability to snap off and refresh the blade when needed. I use a craft knife along with a ruler when lining drawers. It is the best way to get that nice clean edge. I also use a craft knife when applying wallpaper to furniture. When you want to add wallpaper detail into grooved inserts, the craft knife is perfect for trimming inside

those grooves and making the wallpaper appear seamless with the paint. I recommend keeping a selection of several different craft knives in different shapes and sizes. The smaller retractable-blade knives are perfect for those tight fits when lining the insides of drawers and when applying wallpaper to furniture. With snap-off blades, you can refresh the blade with each cut, which ensures clean cuts. Larger utility knives are the best choice for the more labor-intensive tasks like cutting through cardboard and trimming veneer.

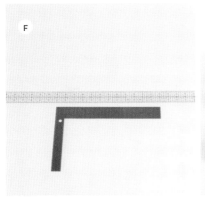

F

G

H

LONG-NOSE PLIERS WITH CUTTER

FIG. C

These are multitasking pliers. I use them all the time, but they are especially helpful when attaching new hardware to furniture. The long nose allows great access to small spaces, and gives you a firm grip on nuts and bolts when tightening or trying to remove any kind of screw. The cutting option in the middle is an added bonus and can be used to cut wire and twine as you work.

METAL FILE

FIG. D

This is a great tool for filing off any sharp edges. Generally after you clip off new knobs and hardware with bolt cutters, you're left with an uneven edge. Smoothing the edge with a metal file will ensure that there are no dangerous jagged points or edges.

ROTARY BLADE AND CUTTING MAT

FIG. E

I thought I had hit the jackpot when I purchased these two tools! They are invaluable for cutting larger pieces of paper and fabric, giving you perfectly straight lines and edges. Just make sure that you only use the rotary blade on the mat surface, as any other unspecified blade will ruin the mat.

RULERS

FIG. F

Rulers are an absolute must for marking off guidelines, and ensuring nice straight edges when lining drawers and cutting wallpaper. I find myself using a square ruler by Zona for most of my furniture projects, and especially for drawer lining. It makes transition from side to corner seamless, and the size is perfect for fitting inside drawers. I also use omnigrid rulers in the 1-by-12-inch size and yardstick size. I always have two or three tape measures placed around the studio, and should probably wear one given how much I am constantly grabbing for it!

SANDERS

FIG. G

Use the orbital and belt sanders for all major prep sanding jobs and sanding sponges for more detailed finish work once the paint finish is complete.

▶ **Belt Sander:** A belt sander is stronger than an orbital sander and will remove layers of paint and whatever else may be covering your piece. I use the orbital sander for 95 percent of my work, but there have been a few times where using a belt sander made removing layers of paint off old doors and furniture pieces much more efficient. It's strong, so you have to keep moving and work fast, or you may just end up with a pile of sawdust at your feet!

▶ **Orbital Sander:** Orbital sanders are essential when sanding and preparing a furniture piece for paint. The circular motion is gentle on your furniture, while removing any surface obstruction. Remember to let the sander do the work! You don't need to bear down, as this will cause the sander to overwork, create a visible sanding pattern, and eat through the finish on the piece. I use this sander on a daily basis.

▶ **Sanding Sponges:** I use sanding sponges in fine and medium grit. They are great for very light sanding and hand distressing. I go through these like candy in the studio. I use fine sanding sponges for all of my hand distressing after the furniture piece has been painted. A medium-grit sanding sponge is great for prep work on a small surface that may not require major sanding with the orbital sander, but it is definitely too harsh to sand a freshly painted surface.

SANDPAPER

There are different types of sandpaper and grit levels. The lower the number, the coarser the grit:

- 40–60 Coarse
- 80–120 Medium
- 150–180 Fine
- 220–240 Very fine
- 280–320 Extra Fine
- 360–600 Super Fine

With the work that I do on furniture, I use 80–240 grit papers and sanding sponges. Always start with the coarsest grit and work your way down to the finest grit for a perfectly smooth and prepared finish.

SCISSORS
FIG. H (SEE PAGE 23)

Choose a pair of craft scissors that can get down and dirty on a daily basis. I use regular kitchen scissors for opening packages, cutting plastic to use as drop cloths, and cutting tape. I have a really special pair that I keep only for cutting beautiful fabrics and ribbon. I also have a pair of scissors just for cutting paper when I am working on paper and wallpaper projects. The brand I prefer for my fabric and paper scissors is Fiskar.

SQUEEGEE

This is a small, hard, plastic tool used for smoothing during wallpaper applications and when applying vinyl designs to furniture. This little tool is not flashy, but it is essential for getting smooth paper and vinyl applications on furniture as well as for pushing and smoothing wallpaper into tight corners and crevices.

STEEL WOOL

Steel wool is a mass of very fine, soft steel filaments used to finish, repair, and polish wood. I personally do not use steel wool for sanding, but rather during the stripping process to remove all residue and buildup on the surface of the furniture. I only use #0000 steel wool when working on my furniture projects—it is the perfect

amount of coarseness. The main reason that I do not use it to sand paint finishes is that the iron in the steel wool reacts with wood and leaves a bluish gray stain behind.

WIRE BRUSH

The stainless-steel bristles of this brush are chemical resistant and perfect for removing paint and rust from the surface of furniture. Just be careful that you do not apply too much pressure and damage the wood of the piece you are working on. I use a wire brush for getting into the hard-to-reach places when stripping paint off of furniture, but you can also use this brush for dirt and rust removal as well.

REPAIRS

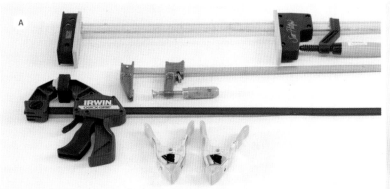

CLAMPS
FIG. A

You will need both metal spring clamps and ratchet bar clamps for repairing and gluing furniture pieces. Clamps apply pressure to keep the structure stable throughout the drying process. Bar clamps are great for keeping drawers straight and tight while gluing and they apply pressure to both sides of the piece being clamped. They extend to different lengths in order to accommodate different-size clamp jobs. Spring clamps apply pressure to both sides as well but are limited to surfaces that are relatively thin since they only open a few inches. Spring clamps are perfect when you need multiple clamps in a small area of width and length. Most spring and bar clamps come with rubber tips on the ends for protecting the surface of the wood, but another way to protect the wood of your furniture while clamping is to use a scrap piece of wood as a

barrier between the furniture surface and the clamp. I suggest keeping a few different sizes of clamps on hand. With the metal spring clamps, I find the most use for the 2- and 3-inch sizes, and with the bar clamps you will need a 12-inch and a 24-inch.

COMPRESSOR
FIG. B

A compressor is an attachment that provides a power source for your nail and staple guns. I can't say how much I enjoy this tool—I always feel like "She Woman" when I use it! A compressor and nail gun combo makes attaching new furniture backing and repairs fast and efficient.

CORDLESS DRILL
FIG. C (SEE PAGE 26)

A cordless drill is essential for drilling new hardware holes, removing old hardware, and tightening up joint screws.

Just be sure to keep it charged because this is one of those tools you will use over and over for multiple projects and techniques. The drill that I use comes with an assortment of bits attached to it, and the two bits that I use most often are the flat head and the Phillips head. I also use spade bits for router jobs and I make sure that I have my pilot-point drill bit set handy for drilling new hardware holes.

MASK OR RESPIRATOR
FIG. D (SEE PAGE 26)

Be sure to wear a mask or respirator when sanding, spray-painting, or applying any chemicals. A dust mask is best used during sanding and cleaning. A respirator should be used when working with harsh chemicals, when using a paint sprayer, and when working with spray paint. Always read and follow the safety precautions and instructions on products before you start.

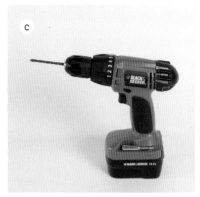

C

D

E

F

G

H

NAIL GUN AND STAPLE GUN
FIGS. E, F

Nail and staple guns are used in conjunction with the air compressor. These are two tools that I can't live without! Nail guns turn bigger jobs like building work tables, adding new backing to furniture, and stability repairs into quick and easy jobs. One click of the trigger and your nail is in before you can blink. Nail and staple sizes vary depending on the job, and can be purchased at your local hardware store. I use nail and staple guns for replacing drawers, applying backing, small repairs, attaching upholstery, and much more.

PAINTER'S TOOL
FIG. G

This is a multipurpose tool that can be used as a putty spatula, paint can opener, roller cleaner, hammer, scraper, spreader, and even nail remover. This tool is a must-have for anyone in the furniture-painting business.

SAFETY GLASSES

Safety glasses come in all shapes and sizes and colors. It doesn't matter what style or color you choose as long as you wear them! Safety glasses protect your eyes from dust and flying debris while sanding, and chemicals or splatters while painting.

PUTTY SPATULAS
FIG. H

Spackle spatulas come in handy for applying wood filler and Bondo, and I use them on a daily basis in my furniture work. These spatulas are the best tool for making your fills and repairs perfectly smooth. I do not recommend using anything else. Make sure to clean your spatulas well when finished in order to keep them in smooth working order.

MISCELLANEOUS

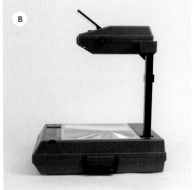

DEGREASER/CLEANER
FIG. A

Krud Kutter is a nontoxic, biodegradable cleaner and degreaser that removes oil paint, rust, wax, tar . . . you name it! I use this product all the time to remove sticky substances inside drawers, clean out paintbrushes, and remove general dirt and grime.

OVERHEAD PROJECTOR
FIG. B

This is a very old-school tool that is not used a whole lot anymore. But when used with a printed transparency, an overhead projector provides endless design opportunities. I use an overhead projector to trace designs onto the surface of furniture. I then go back and hand-paint the traced designs. This a great tool for those of us who cannot freehand elaborate designs!

VACUUM

I use a regular upright vacuum with attachments in the studio. I did have a shop vac at one time, and then someone borrowed it and it never returned! Oops! I have found, though, that I love just a regular upright vacuum with attachments. The brush attachment is great for cleaning furniture surfaces and removing dust after sanding, and the long narrow attachment is perfect for getting into all the cracks and crevices and removing dirt and cobwebs.

HARDWARE

The hardware you choose for your piece can make or break the final outcome. Whether you choose to keep the original hardware or change it out for something new is totally up to you, but having a vision from the beginning will help you make the right choice. Think about the look you are after. Whether it is French, modern, retro, glam, eclectic, whimsical, or rustic, you will need to keep that in mind when selecting hardware. You want the piece to have a cohesive look. For instance, when trying to achieve a rustic modern look, you would not want to choose a ceramic flower knob or a glass knob with polka dots. Instead you would want to choose a wooden, bone, or metallic knob to go with the overall design. Hardware stores carry some great wooden knobs that can be painted and customized, and stores like Anthropologie and Hobby Lobby are great sources for all different styles of knobs and pulls. I have been known to pick up knobs in specialty stores while on vacation. You never know when you will stumble on a good set of hardware!

BONE

FIG. A

Most bone knobs come in shades of either cream or brown and work well for a modern rustic look. Bone adds classic beauty without distracting from the piece itself. I use bone knobs most often when working on subtly colored pieces like grays, blacks, and driftwoods, to give them an extra touch of earthiness and a soft rustic feel.

CERAMIC

FIG. B

Ceramic knobs offer the widest range of colors and patterns. I use ceramic hardware the most in my furniture pieces. The options are seemingly endless—flower shapes, stripes, fluted forms, painted artwork, polka dots, letters, and numbers. Ceramic knobs provide several different design looks, from whimsical to classic, and come in a variety of shapes and sizes.

GLASS

FIG. C

Glass comes in many shapes and sizes and adds a pretty shimmer to furniture. Sometimes glass knobs can create unique illusions because of their transparent nature, depending on the color of paint chosen for the piece. Keep this in mind as you coordinate colors and patterns. I tend to prefer round glass knobs, just because that is how my brain is wired, but there are many shapes and sizes to choose from. My favorite glass knobs are about the size of a tennis ball. I love these particular knobs because they grab your attention at first look: I have yet to find a piece that they do not look great on. Glass knobs are great for adding classic and feminine details to furniture.

METAL

FIG. D

Metallic knobs are great for adding a glamorous look to a piece of furniture. I love to pair metallic silver, gold, and gemstone hardware with wallpapered furniture pieces. There is just something about rhinestones and shiny metal on furniture that is instantly charming and inviting.

ORIGINAL HARDWARE

Sometimes the original hardware is absolutely perfect for the piece, and can be left as-is or simply painted in a complementary shade. In my work, I rarely use the original hardware, though, because most of the time it does not match the look I'm after, but every now and again I come across a piece with gorgeous hardware. When this happens, I make sure to include it in the design.

RESIN AND ROPE

FIG. E

Jute or rope knobs are great for a casual, beachy feel or a Swedish look. Sometimes just taking strips of fabric or rope and looping them through the hardware holes in a series of knots is all you need to finish off the piece you are working on. Resin knobs are also great for a casual and whimsical addition to your furniture pieces. Synthetic resin is a hard moldable plastic that comes in many shapes and sizes. Resin knobs can be used on multiple styles of pieces due to the wide variety of choices available.

WOOD

FIG. F

Wood knobs are truly beautiful in their raw form. The woodgrain patterns and organic shapes are great additions to projects on the more traditional side. I find myself pairing wooden knobs with milk-paint pieces a lot. I love the outdoor, woodsy feel of that combination. Also, unfinished wooden knobs are easy to customize with paint or paper for a unique look.

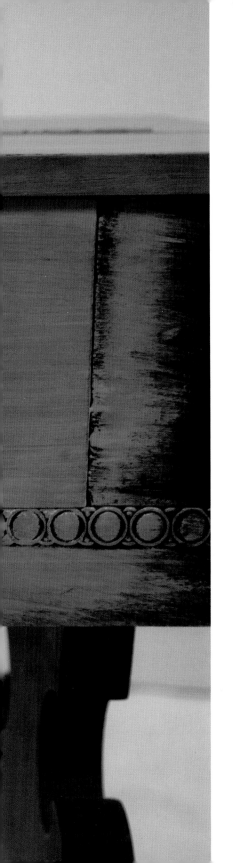

TECHNIQUES

This section features my favorite go-to refinishing techniques that can be applied on many different styles of furniture. I haven't presented these as specific step-by-step projects in the hopes that you will use the techniques to create your own designs on the furniture piece of your choosing. Plus, I know all too well that when working with antique furniture or flea market finds, no two pieces are exactly alike! The breakdown of steps and how-to photos will allow you to replicate these techniques yet apply them in a way that best suits the particular piece you're working on. So embrace your inner artist and get ready to create your very own masterpiece!

STRIPPING
FURNITURE

I know that just the thought of stripping a piece of furniture makes some people cringe! Stripping furniture can be a messy, labor-intensive project, but it is not as daunting as you may think. With products like Citristrip (see page 17), which is a natural stripping agent, the job is much easier and safer than it used to be. Stripping down furniture is not something that I have to do on a regular basis, but every now and then I just can't pass up a piece of furniture that has multiple layers of paint, knowing it could be a beauty.

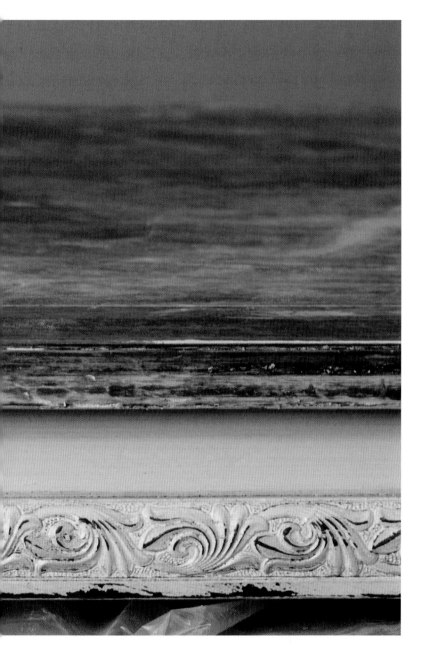

MATERIALS

NEWSPAPER and HEAVY PLASTIC
  (see tip)

CHEMICAL-RESISTANT GLOVES

SAFETY GLASSES

CITRISTRIP

TWO DISPOSABLE TRAYS: one for
  stripping agent and one for the
  After Wash

PAINTBRUSH, Purdy Nylox

PLASTIC PUTTY SPATULA, WIRE
  BRUSH, and TOOTHPICKS
  (if stripping paint)

#0000 STEEL WOOL

SHOP TOWELS

AFTER WASH

ORBITAL SANDER, fine sanding pad

SANDING SPONGE, fine grit

VACUUM

continued . . .

TIP ▶ When working with stripper inside, make sure that the floor underneath your work is chemical resistant! If not, the stripper and After Wash will eat through and damage the floor. Use newspaper and heavy plastic to protect the floor and make for easier cleanup. Stripping furniture is a very messy job, and should be done in an area that can handle the mess.

TIP ▶ Be sure to read the back of the Citristrip and After Wash containers for all safety and application procedures. Follow safety instructions completely, and dispose of all trash according to local state regulations.

1 ▶ **LAY DOWN NEWSPAPER** and heavy plastic on the floor where you will be working. Put on your chemical-resistant gloves and eye protection. Pour a generous amount of Citristrip into a disposable tray and grab your paintbrush to begin. Apply the Citristrip liberally to ensure proper coverage of the surface area being stripped. At first, I thought that since Citristrip was a natural product it would take longer to work, but it actually works relatively quickly. Depending on the surface you are stripping, it may be ready to scrape in 30 minutes, or it could take as long as 24 hours, depending on what is on the surface that you are trying to strip. In my experience, though, a couple of hours is all it takes for the stripper to do its job of softening varnish or bubbling the paint right up.

FIG. A

2 ▶ **PAINT:** When stripping a painted surface, you will know it is ready when the paint slides off easily when pushed with the scraping tool. There should not be a need for intense scraping and pushing. If the paint does not come

FIG. B

off easily, reapply the stripper and wait until the paint is completely ready for removal. Be careful when scraping that you do not gouge the wood of your piece. If the piece is nice and flat, use a plastic spatula to remove paint. For details, nooks, and crannies, you will want to have a small wire brush and toothpicks on hand for getting paint out of all of the grooves.

FIGS. C ▶ **VARNISH:** When stripping off a varnish, like the piece here, apply the stripper and wait 1 hour. It is harder to tell when the varnish is ready because it does not bubble up. The sign that I always look for with varnish is that the stripping agent, which is normally orange, turns brown as it becomes saturated with the varnish stain. Use the steel wool and firmly "sand," following the grain of the wood, to remove the stripper. Steel wool works great on varnishes, and conforms to detailed surfaces nicely. Just be sure to wear chemical-resistant gloves to protect your hands from both the chemicals and the abrasive metal of the steel wool. After the first coat has been removed, you may feel

like you need to reapply a second coat of strip-per. Go ahead and do so, repeat the waiting time, and then sand down the second treat-ment with the steel wool.

3 ▶ **WHEN YOU ARE SATISFIED** with the color of the wood, and feel like all of the paint and/or varnish have been removed, use the second disposable tray and a shop towel to apply the After Wash to remove any lingering chemi-cals. I use steel wool for this process as well, because I feel like it is the best for really get-ting into the surface and removing residue. Be careful not to oversaturate the wood with the After Wash. Avoid puddles of After Wash on the surface of your piece.

4 ▶ **LET THE PIECE DRY COMPLETELY.** This may take 1 to 2 hours, depending on the temperature of the room and the saturation of the piece. Once the piece is completely dry to the touch, you can begin sanding. For heavier sanding on flat surfaces, use an orbital

FIG. D

sander with a fine sanding pad and work in light motions in the direction of the wood grain. I prefer to use a fine sanding sponge for detailed sanding, such as turned legs or carved wood cutouts, in order to preserve the integrity of the wood. Sand until the wood is completely smooth to the touch.

5 ▶ **VACUUM THE ENTIRE PIECE** to remove all sanding dust and wipe it down with a clean shop towel to ensure a nice smooth and clean surface.

FIG. E

6 ▶ **THE PIECE IS NOW READY FOR PAINTING** or a new stain finish.

SANDING
FURNITURE

Sanding is a key step to ensuring a beautiful and long-lasting paint job, so make sure that you do not ever skip out on this part of the process! Proper sanding removes build-up, dirt, surface scratches, and shiny finishes that may affect the final look you're after.

MATERIALS

SHOP TOWELS

PUTTY SPATULA

WOOD FILLER

ORBITAL SANDER,
fine sanding pad

DUST MASK

SAFETY GLASSES

SANDPAPER, various grits

SANDING SPONGES, fine and
medium grit

VACUUM

1 ▶ **WHEN YOU START** working on your piece of furniture, it is a good idea to take note of repairs that need to take place prior to sanding. I like to give the piece a rundown with a barely damp shop towel to remove the initial dirt and cobwebs. Then, I dry off the piece with a clean dry towel.

2 ▶ **IF THERE ARE ANY SMALL SCRATCHES,** dings, or missing veneer chips in your piece, you will want to go ahead and use a putty spatula to fill those with wood filler before sanding. This is also the time to fill any unwanted hardware holes with wood filler as well.

3 ▶ **ONCE ALL OF THE WOOD FILLER HAS DRIED,** you are ready to begin sanding down the entire piece. Drying times will vary depending on the extent of the fill. Most surface scratches and shallow fills are dry enough to sand after 1 hour.

4 ▶ **THE FIRST RULE TO REMEMBER** in sanding is to *always sand with the grain of the wood.* Not doing this will cause lines and circular scratches in your finish. For flat surfaces like drawer fronts, tops, and sides, it is easiest to sand with an orbital sander. Using an orbital

FIG. A

sander will take much less time than hand sanding, and will leave the surface in better condition for accepting paint. Be sure to wear a dust mask and safety glasses when using an orbital sander to protect your face from flying debris. Let the sander do the work for you, and do not press into the wood. Pressing too hard will cause the sander to overwork, and damage the surface of the piece. Be sure that you use a very fine sanding pad when doing prep sanding so that you do not eat all the way through the finish down to the bare wood. Ninety-five percent of the pieces I choose to refinish need just a light overall sanding that is noninvasive to the existing finish. If you sand too harshly, you will sand right through the entire finish, which will show up as dull patches in your paint finish—not what you want to happen! Sand just enough to remove any dirt or grime, and give the paint a good gripping surface.

5 ▶ **WHEN YOU NEED TO DO A DEEPER SAND-ING,** it is important to choose the right sand-paper grit for each step. You will want to start out with a coarse grit and work your way to a

fine grit. Each level removes the lines from the previous sanding until the surface is smooth and perfect for painting or refinishing.

6 ▶ **FOR DETAILED CARVINGS,** turned legs, and tight corners, it is really important to hand sand. I choose to use sanding sponges because they contour to both my hand and the shape of whatever I am sanding. An orbital sander is just too strong for these areas and can damage carved detail beyond repair.

....
FIG. B

7 ▶ **FINALLY, USE YOUR HANDS!** When com-pleting a sanding job, I always close my eyes and run my fingers over the areas that I have sanded to see if they pass the "feel test"! It is amazing how sensitive your sense of touch is. This is the best way to discover any lingering roughness.

8 ▶ **VACUUM THE ENTIRE PIECE** to remove all sanding dust and wipe down with a damp shop towel to ensure a nice smooth and clean surface before applying the paint finish.

....
FIG. C

SMALL REPAIRS

Repairs are not the most fun aspect of the refinishing process because they can seem tedious and uncreative, but they are the key to a professional and well-applied finish. Take your time, do them right, and it will make all the difference in the end result of your furniture projects.

- WOOD FILLING
- GLUING & CLAMPING
- ROUTER RETROFITS FOR NEW HARDWARE

WOOD FILLING

Most vintage hardware uses two holes, and with my furniture projects I like to use knobs instead of handles, so that leaves me with an extra hole. Sometimes you will only need to fill one of the existing holes depending on placement, but most of the time you have to cover both holes and drill a new hole in the center of the drawer. Make sure you fill the existing holes and drill new holes before painting. It is much easier to measure off and drill new holes when you can use the existing holes as a guideline for centering.

MATERIALS

WOOD FILLER, paintable and stainable
PUTTY SPATULA
SANDING SPONGE, fine grit
SHOP TOWELS

1 **USING YOUR WOOD FILLER** and putty spatula, fill any unwanted holes, then very lightly smooth over the surface with your spatula. You will be applying a second coat, so work on getting this first fill as full and smooth as you can. You will want to scrape off all the excess putty surrounding the hole so that it does not create a ridge in your finish, or cause you to sand through the finish surrounding the hole.

FIG. A

2 **ALLOW THE WOOD FILLER TO DRY** completely. The deeper the hole, the longer it will take to dry. Shallow fills take 30 minutes to an hour to dry, while deeper fills may need 3 to 4 hours to dry completely.

3 **ONCE THE FIRST COAT OF FILLER IS DRY,** sand it completely smooth with a fine sanding sponge before applying the second coat.

4 **APPLY THE SECOND COAT OF FILLER** exactly as the first and remove any excess surrounding the repair area. This fill will be very shallow and will dry quickly. You want this fill to be the final fill, so be sure that it is very smooth.

FIG. B

5 **ONCE THE SECOND FILL IS DRY,** sand it lightly again with the sanding sponge to smooth. If you have done the filling correctly, it will not show in your painted finish at all. Make sure it is completely smooth and flat before applying paint.

FIG. C

6 **USE A LIGHTLY DAMP SHOP TOWEL** to wipe the surface of the furniture and remove all sanding dust.

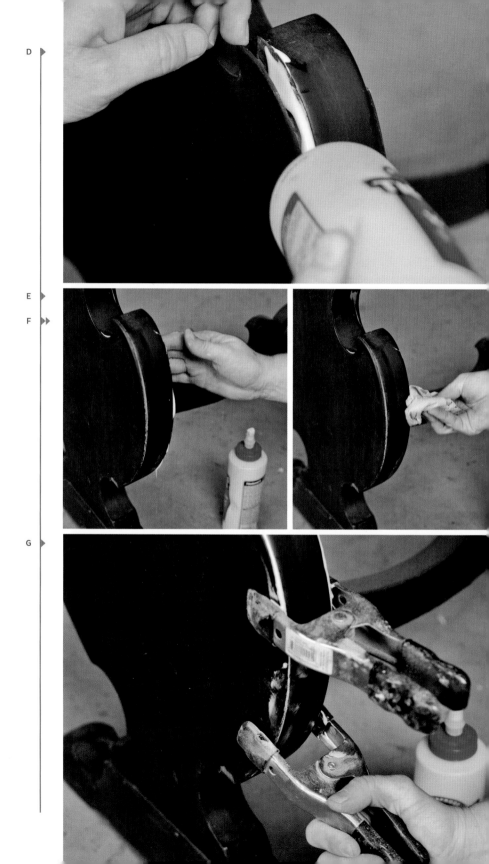

D ▶

E ▶

F ▶▶

G ▶

GLUING & CLAMPING

Whether it is repairing damaged veneer or gluing rickety joints back together, the most important thing to remember when doing this kind of repair is that all of the pieces should fit together perfectly and smoothly. If the joint and veneer are uneven or disjoined in any way, it will compromise the integrity of both the furniture piece and the repair.

MATERIALS

WOOD GLUE

SMALL PAINTBRUSH (optional)

CLAMPS, spring and bar types

SHOP TOWELS

SANDING SPONGE OR PAPER

1 ▶
....
FIG. D

WHEN REPAIRING LOOSE VENEER, place an even amount of glue underneath the surface, so that the entire surface is covered. Be very careful when lifting and repairing loose veneer. If you lift too harshly it will crack and break, so work gently and cautiously to avoid further damaging the veneer. If you use a small paintbrush to spread the glue, this will keep your fingers a little bit cleaner! I don't mind dirty fingers, so I use my hands. If you are repairing any loose joints, make sure both pieces fit together perfectly before you apply the glue. If they do not fit together, no matter how much glue you use, the piece will not be structurally sound. Apply the glue to both pieces.

2 ▶
....
FIG. E

PRESS THE AREAS YOU ARE GLUING together tightly and apply pressure with the spring clamps or bar clamps, depending on the surface being clamped.

3 ▶
....
FIG. F

USE TOWELS to wipe off any excess glue that seeps out when the clamp pressure is applied.

4 ▶
....
FIG. G

WOOD GLUE NEEDS A GOOD BIT OF TIME to dry. Leave it clamped and in a stable position for the full drying time. I usually leave my repairs to dry for 48 hours. If you missed wiping any glue and find you have some hard dried glue on the surface of your piece, lightly sand the glue off the surface before continuing and painting.

ROUTER RETROFITS FOR NEW HARDWARE

I use this technique when I have my heart set on a certain knob but, alas, the drawer front is too thick and the screw is not long enough to come through the other side for attachment. The purpose of this technique is to make the back side of the drawer thinner so that the hardware that was once too short will now come through and you can attach a washer and bolt.

MATERIALS

SPADE BIT, 1 inch

CORDLESS DRILL

VACUUM

1 ▶ **PLACE THE SPADE BIT** into the cordless drill (make sure it is screwed in tight!).

FIG. H

2 ▶ **PLACE THE DRAWER** on a flat surface, front side down.

3 ▶ **PUT THE POINT OF THE SPADE BIT** into the existing hardware hole on the inside of the drawer, and bore into the wood. Be very careful that you do not drill all the way through to the front of the drawer! Depending on the thickness of the wood, the depth varies. Usually about a half inch is the deepest you will need to drill.

FIG. I

4 ▶ **VACUUM UP ALL OF THE WOOD SHAVINGS,** and apply the new hardware.

FIGS. J

PRIMING
FURNITURE

I have a love-hate relationship with primer! I am a bit unconventional when it comes to using primer. If I am going for a distressed look on a piece of furniture, I do not prime the furniture because the primer only negates what I am trying to achieve with the finish. I do, however, prime pieces that I know will get a high level of usage, like dining room tables and sinks; knotted wood, as those knots will show through the paint finish without a coat of primer to block them; and pieces that have a redwood or mahogany finish that tends to bleed through the paint once the surface has been disturbed. When I choose to use a primer, I only use Benjamin Moore Stix Waterborne bonding primer and have it tinted at the store in the color that I will be painting the piece of furniture. When priming a mahogany or redwood finish piece, you will need to use a primer that has a stain blocker as well. Before you start, make sure that the piece of furniture you are getting ready to prime is sanded (see Sanding Furniture, page 36, and Figs. A), vacuumed, and wiped clean with a shop towel. You do not want any dust or dirt to remain on the surface.

MATERIALS

ORBITAL SANDER, fine sanding pad

VACCUUM

PRIMER

PAINT TRAY

FOAM ROLLER

PAINTBRUSH, Purdy Nylox

SANDING SPONGE, fine grit

SHOP TOWELS

1 ▶ **SAND LIGHTLY** with an orbital sander and be sure to vacuum the sanding dust up and wipe the surface clean with a damp cloth.

....
FIGS. A

2 ▶ **POUR SOME PRIMER** into a paint tray and roll the foam roller in the paint until it is evenly saturated. It does not need to be dripping, just evenly coated.

3 ▶ **IF YOU ARE WORKING ON A DETAILED SUR-FACE,** use a paintbrush to insure that all of the tight spots are covered. Otherwise, use a foam roller for all flat and angled surfaces.

4 ▶ **APPLY A THIN COAT OF PRIMER,** making sure to coat the surface smoothly and evenly. Allow the first coat to dry completely, 3 to 4 hours or according to the manufacturer's instructions.

....
FIG. B

5 ▶ **IF THE FIRST COAT IS SMOOTH** and even with no spotty appearance, you can stop at one coat. If the finish is uneven in color, go ahead and sand lightly with a fine sanding sponge and be sure to vacuum the sanding dust up and wipe the surface clean with a damp cloth.

6 ▶ **APPLY A SECOND COAT** of primer exactly as you applied the first. Once the second coat is dry, you are free to begin painting your piece of furniture.

APPLYING
POLYURETHANE

Polyurethane is one of the most durable and easy-to-apply protective finishes for your furniture projects. Polyurethanes are available in both oil-based and water-based formulas. For furniture pieces that will see a lot of wear and tear, few finishes are as appropriate as polyurethane for the final coating. I use water-based polyurethane for the majority of my work, but there are pieces like dining room tables and furniture pieces that are intended for use with sinks that I will only coat with oil-based polyurethane. There is one oil-based brand that I use by General Finishes called Arm-R-Seal Oil & Urethane Top-coat. The instructions following work for water- and oil-based polyurethanes.

MATERIALS

POLYURETHANE

STIR STICK

PAINT TRAY

PAINTBRUSH, Purdy White China
   Brush Series

SANDPAPER, 220 grit, or
   SANDING SPONGE, fine grit

VACUUM

SHOP TOWELS

continued . . .

1 ▶ **WHETHER YOU ARE WORKING** with an oil-based or water-based polyurethane, be sure that you are working in a well-ventilated and well-lit area.

2 ▶ **OPEN THE CAN OF POLYURETHANE** and stir it well with a stir stick. Never shake a can of polyurethane, as this will create bubbles that will show up in your finish.

3 ▶ **POUR THE POLYURETHANE** into a paint tray. This will keep any dust or dirt particles picked up by the brush from getting into the can of polyurethane and contaminating the rest of the product.

4 ▶ **MAKE SURE YOU HAVE A HIGH-QUALITY BRUSH** for applying stains and clears (aka polyurethanes). This will make a huge difference in the outcome of your finish. Inexpensive synthetic-bristle brushes will leave obvious brush strokes in your finish. Dip your brush into the polyurethane and gently tap it against the side of the tray. Tap instead of drag it, so that more product will stay on the brush and give your piece a more even finish.

5 ▶ **USE LONG, EVEN STROKES,** following the grain of the wood and avoid overworking the product. Overworking, which is another name for overbrushing, will cause an uneven finish. You want to complete each pass in one long stroke. It is best to wait until the first coat dries completely and then go back and sand and reapply.

FIGS. A

6 ▶ **MAKE SURE THAT YOU COVER** the entire surface evenly—this is why it is important to work in a well-lit area. If necessary, shine a light onto the surface you are working on to make sure you've covered everything.

7 ▶ **ONCE THE ENTIRE SURFACE IS COVERED,** allow it to dry completely. Drying times vary depending on the product you are using, so be sure to read the label and follow the manufacturer's directions carefully. Some polyurethanes will dry in as little as 1 to 2 hours, while others can take up to 24 hours.

8 ▶ **ONCE YOU HAVE LET THE FIRST COAT DRY** completely, sand the entire surface with fine sandpaper or a fine sanding sponge. Use light pressure to even out the surface before applying the second coat. Be careful not to sand harshly through the first layer of polyurethane.

....
FIG. B

9 ▶ **VACUUM THE ENTIRE SURFACE** and use a damp shop towel to wipe down after sanding. Any leftover dust particles will cause roughness in your finish, so make sure that you remove it all from the surface.

10 ▶ **APPLY A TOTAL OF THREE TO FOUR COATS** of polyurethane, following the preceding drying and sanding instructions for each coat. This will complete your finish, and provide great durability and protection.

....
FIG. C

PAINTING
FURNITURE

Paint has magical powers, and wipes the slate clean for a tired piece of furniture that has seen better days. All it takes is a little time and sweat equity to create a piece that is full of personality and character. Proper prep work is what makes a good paint finish stand out in the crowd. Before you start, look over the piece thoroughly and make any necessary repairs. Sand (see page 36), wood fill (see page 40), and glue (see page 42) any and all areas that could create problems in either the finish or functionality of the piece. (If you are going to be using new hardware, you will need to drill new holes.)

MATERIALS

ORBITAL SANDER, SANDPAPER,
  and/or SANDING SPONGE

VACUUM

SHOP TOWELS

GREEN FROGTAPE

PAINT

PAINT TRAY

FOAM ROLLER

PAINTBRUSHES: Purdy Nylox brushes
  for paint and White China Brush
  Series brush for finish

PLASTIC GLOVES

STAIN, WAX, or POLYURETHANE

continued . . .

1 ▶
FIG. A
ONCE ALL OF THE REPAIRS ARE MADE, sand the entire piece (see page 36). It is safe to use an orbital sander, sandpaper, or a sanding sponge, but be extremely careful to sand the piece evenly and properly. Once the sanding is complete, vacuum the entire piece and wipe it down with a clean damp shop towel to remove all dust particles.

2 ▶
FIG. B
WHEN ALL THE DUST IS REMOVED, tape off the edges of the piece with the FrogTape. I usually tape off any part of the furniture that I do not want to get any paint on. These areas are the sides of the drawers, drawer runners, casters, and the interior of the cabinet, where you want nice clean paint lines. This is one of those steps that some choose to skip over, but I believe this is a must! There is nothing like seeing a beautiful, clean, straight edge versus messy, sloppy paint overage (for instance, when you slide open one of the drawers of your furniture piece only to find yourself staring at paint slopped on the side of the drawer instead of a nice clean line that shows intent and purpose). It is the difference between professional and amateur, and I am dead serious about that!

3 ▶
FIGS. C
NOW, YOU ARE READY TO PAINT! Pour the paint in the painting tray and roll the foam roller in the paint to get it nice and coated. Just make sure that the roller has plenty of paint on the entire surface so that it will paint evenly. There is no need for an excess of paint on the roller; a lot of paint will just create more work for you, as you have to work to smooth it out and wipe away paint that has crept around the edges. Use the foam roller for all the large, flat surfaces, and Nylox brushes for cutting in corners and trim work. The foam roller gives the smoothest finish for a hand finish, and it makes the work

go quickly. Just be sure that you check all of the edges for paint overage, and be sure to fix any overages while the paint is wet to keep from having those unsightly ripples and drips in the finish.

4 ▶
ALLOW THE FIRST COAT TO DRY completely before applying the second coat. Apply the second coat exactly like the first coat.

5 ▶
FIG. D
WHEN THE PAINT IS COMPLETELY DRY, and you want a distressed finish, it is time to sand (again). It can take some paints several hours to dry properly, so make sure you read the directions and follow accordingly. If you would like a really distressed look, use an orbital sander. If you choose a lighter, more hand-done distressed finish, use a fine sanding sponge. The goal here is to create an authentic and timeless look, so be careful to avoid large distressing "holes" or gouges, which are very harsh, or unnatural spots in the paint finish. A good rule of thumb is to distress hard edges, protruding detail, curves, around the hardware, edges of drawers, and any areas that would normally get lots of usage markings.

6 ▶
FIG. E
AFTER SANDING, VACUUM AGAIN to remove all the sanding dust. Wearing gloves, apply the finish of choice, whether it is a stain, wax, or polyurethane (see pages 56, 58, and 48).

7 ▶
ONCE THE FINISH IS COMPLETELY DRY, attach your new hardware, line the drawers with paper, or paint the insides of the drawers, and you are ready to enjoy your new piece!

A

B

C

D

E

STAINING
OVER PAINT

Staining over paint finishes is a favorite trick of mine, even though most people use glazes, and I'll tell you why: Stains give you way more workability time than glazes, and in my humble opinion, a more authentic finish. Nothing against glazes; it's just that in my experience—because of how fast glaze dries—it does not blend as well and can look heavy-handed, whereas a stain gives you time to really blend well and has a more translucent finish. Before starting, make sure your furniture piece is painted (see page 52), sanded (see page 36), and completely ready for the finish to be applied.

MATERIALS

PLASTIC GLOVES

STAIN

PAINTBRUSH, Purdy White China Brush Series

SHOP TOWELS

 TIP ▶ Apply stain in manageable sections, so that you do not get ahead of yourself and end up with heavier applications in the areas you couldn't get to fast enough. The longer the stain sits on top of the finish, the darker it will be, so make sure to take that into account. Don't apply the stain to the entire piece, and then go back and start wiping it down. Where you started will be darker than where you finished. To ensure an even finish, apply in one area, wipe, and then go on to the next area.

A ◄   1 ►
....
FIG. A

WEARING GLOVES, apply the stain with a brush (I like to use a China brush because of the soft bristles that do not leave ridges or lines behind in the finish), making sure that you cover the area entirely. Most of the stain will get wiped away, but what needs to stay will settle in all the right places.

2 ►
....
FIGS. B

ONCE THE STAIN COMPLETELY COVERS the surface, let it stand for 2 to 3 minutes, and then wipe down that section completely with a shop towel. Be sure to wipe in the direction of the grain, not in circular motions, as that will show up in the final finish. Use your creative eye to determine when the finish is right. Look for areas that may appear heavier than others, or a little bit forced. Go back and soften those areas by smoothing them with your rag so they blend better. The key is to create a look that is timeless, and not contrived. It is perfectly okay to let the stain settle where dirt and time would naturally appear over years of use. The drying time for stains over paint can seem long. It usually takes 3 to 4 days in a controlled temperature to lose the "tacky" feel, and get completely dry. It is so worth it though, I promise!

B ◄

WAXING
OVER PAINT

Wax is a beautiful and durable finish for both painted and unpainted furniture. Wax gives a completely different look than polyurethane and stain. It produces an aged, more muted shine to furniture compared to the higher shines of stains and polyurethanes. It is also a little more difficult to apply. You need to work quickly to ensure that the finish is smooth and authentic looking. Wax is my finish of choice when I want to add natural age and depth to a piece without adding a lot of shine. Before you start, make sure your furniture piece is painted (see page 52) and ready for the waxing process.

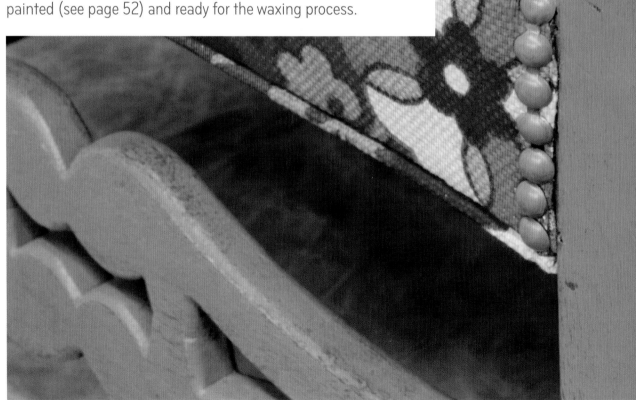

MATERIALS

SANDING SPONGE, fine grit

PLASTIC GLOVES

WAX BRUSH OR PAINTBRUSH,
  Purdy White China Brush Series

WAXES, clear and dark (see tip)

SHOP TOWELS

continued . . .

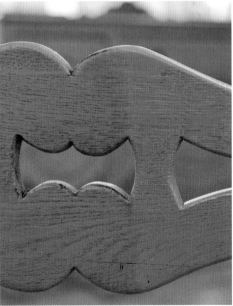

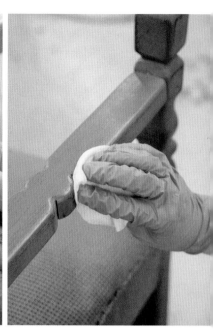

TIP ▶ A great tool for buffing your way to a beautiful shine is to use an old pair of tights or pantyhose for buffing.

TIP ▶ Dark wax can be extremely hard to blend when applied too heavily to the surface of furniture, so I recommend mixing a dark wax with a clear wax for easier blending and a consistent finish. Wax dries very quickly, so the workability time is limited. Work in sections, and work fast!

1 ▶ **LIGHTLY SAND THE WOOD** with a fine sanding sponge (wearing gloves while sanding is optional).

FIG. A

2 ▶ **WEARING GLOVES AND USING A WAX BRUSH** or China brush, apply the wax one section at a time. Dip the brush in the clear wax, and then lightly dip it into the dark wax. (I do the mixing right in the can because it is so minimal, but if you are worried about muddying up your clear wax, you can take a little bit of each color out in separate containers for your mixing.) It is

FIG. B

better to have a 2-to-1 ratio of clear to dark for the best results. The key with wax is to apply it sparingly and evenly.

3 ▶ **WORK THE WAX BACK AND FORTH** in the small section you are working on until you are happy with the shading and depth of the finish. It does not matter where you start on the piece of furniture, but I tend to start on the sides and work my way around, leaving the top for last. There is no specific rule; that is just what I find works best for me. The important thing is to work in sections. Have some shop towels on hand for blending, in case you get a little heavy-handed. Do not stress if you end up with a heavy spot; you can always go back with a sanding sponge and blend.

4 ▶ **ALLOW THE WAX TO DRY** (drying times vary, so follow the manufacturer's instructions). The particular wax that I use dries in minutes, so you can begin buffing almost immediately. The typical sign that the wax is dry and ready for buffing is that it appears cloudy or completely flat in appearance. Buff with a shop towel until you achieve that beautiful matte shine you are after.

FIG. C

REFRESHING WOOD WITH
DANISH OIL

Sometimes a design plan calls for leaving some of the natural wood as is. I like to do this especially when working on mid-century pieces that have beautiful wooden legs. The wood may have become scratched or dull over time; Danish oil is a great way to freshen up the wood and make it look new again. Applying Danish oil is a quick and easy process.

MATERIALS

SANDING SPONGE, fine grit

SHOP TOWELS

PLASTIC GLOVES

DANISH OIL

PAINTBRUSH, Purdy White China
    Brush Series

1 ▶ **LIGHTLY SAND THE WOOD** with a fine sanding sponge (wearing gloves while sanding is optional). Be careful not to sand too harshly—you don't want to disturb the finish.

FIG. A

2 ▶ **WIPE DOWN THE SURFACE** after sanding with a damp shop towel in order to remove all sanding dust and dirt.

3 ▶ **WEARING GLOVES, APPLY THE DANISH OIL** with a brush or a shop towel making sure to cover the entire surface. The oil can be applied with a brush or a towel achieving the same results. I prefer application with a shop towel.

FIG. B

4 ▶ **ONCE THE OIL HAS BEEN APPLIED** to the entire surface, wipe off excess oil with a clean dry shop towel.

APPLYING WALLPAPER
TO FURNITURE

Wallpaper is one of my favorite accessories to add to furniture. I was not blessed with great drawing skills, and that is why I think I love wallpaper so much. It creates the illusion of a hand-painted design, and does not discriminate against the lack of both natural ability and an art degree! I use wallpaper on the surface of furniture in my designs, but also inside drawers as a liner. When applying wallpaper to unfinished wood, you will need to prime the wood before the application (see page 46). This ensures that the untreated wood will not soak up all of the wallpaper paste, which could cause adhering issues in the future. It is also really important to sand well, making sure the surface is as smooth as possible (see page 36). The wallpaper will pick up any defects as it dries, and shrink right into those spaces if you are not careful.

MATERIALS

RULER

WALLPAPER

SCISSORS

WALLPAPER PASTE

PAINTBRUSHES: Purdy Nylox brush for paste and White China Brush Series brush for finish

SHOP TOWELS

CRAFT KNIFE

PLASTIC SQUEEGEE

POLYURETHANE, water based

SANDING SPONGE, fine grit

VACUUM

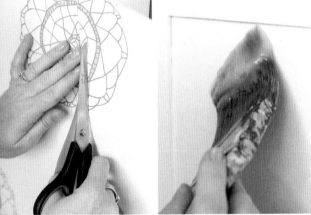

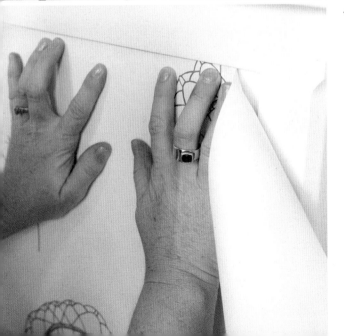

A ◄

FIGS. A

1 ▶ **ONCE THE PIECE IS PRIMED** and painted, begin measuring with a ruler and planning out the wallpaper placement. It is important to know exactly where the paper will be, especially if you are applying a large pattern or stripe; you want the pattern to match up perfectly. Measure out your pieces of paper so that once they are applied to the piece, trimming with scissors is minimal. When your cuts are close to accurate, it makes smoothing the wallpaper and pushing it into the corners much easier than when you have large amounts of excess that just get in your way. I do recommend leaving a little extra length on all sides, about 1 inch, just in case you need to adjust.

◄◄

B ◄

FIG. B

2 ▶ **APPLY THE WALLPAPER PASTE** with a Nylox brush, according to the manufacturer's instructions. With the particular paper I used here, the designer recommended applying the paste to the object rather than the paper. Make sure that the paste is applied smoothly and evenly. Clumps and thick streaks will show up in your paper and cause air bubbles.

3 ▶ **PLACE THE WALLPAPER ON THE SURFACE** of the furniture, being careful to avoid getting paste on the front side of the paper. (It is a good idea to keep lots of shop towels on hand to keep your hands clean.) Smooth the paper with your hands as much as possible, working from top to bottom, smoothing from the center outward to remove all air bubbles. When applying wallpaper to inserts or cutouts, push the paper into the creases and corners nice and tight so that when you trim, your line is very accurate. I like to use a ruler with a nice straight edge to help push the paper into the creases, but be careful not to get too aggressive with this, as it may cause the paper to tear. A good rule to remember when smoothing out air bubbles is to start in the center and work outward.

FIG. C

C ◄

continued . . .

4 ▶
ONCE THE PAPER IS IN PLACE, trim off the excess using a straight-edge or ruler and a craft knife. Always keep the craft knife right next to the edge of the ruler. Do not push down with extreme pressure, as it will cause the paper to ridge and tear. In order to keep nice straight lines, refresh your blade after every cut.

5 ▶ **USE A CLEAN, DAMP CLOTH** to wipe down the entire surface and make sure any and all air bubbles are smoothed out. If you find yourself having a hard time with air bubbles, use a plastic squeegee to smooth down the entire surface. Allow the wallpaper to dry completely, and then apply the first coat of water-based polyurethane, using the China brush (see page 48). When the first coat is dry, usually in about 3 to 4 hours, sand it very lightly with a fine sanding sponge to ensure that the surface is nice and smooth.

6 ▶ **REMOVE ANY SANDING DUST** by vacuuming and wiping down the surface with a clean shop towel. Apply the second coat of polyurethane and let it dry. Remember that paper is paper and prone to ripping or scratching, so use care when deciding on the placement of the wallpaper on your piece. For example, if you choose to apply paper to a desk top, you may want to have a piece of glass cut to protect the surface from wear and tear.

APPLYING
METAL LEAF

Using metal or gold leaf in art has been around in traditional form for hundreds of years. It is traditionally called "gilding," and was used for many years on picture frames, artwork, and jewelry. I tend to be a little on the nontraditional side in my application of metal leaf on furniture, and believe the beauty is in the sparkle and imperfection. Metal leaf is available at any craft or art supply store. Before you start, plan out where you want to apply the metal leafing. You can apply metal leaf to both painted and unpainted surfaces; decide if you want it on top of your painted surface or showing through underneath the painted surface. I have done it both ways, and distressing through the paint and allowing some shimmer to come through is a beautiful way to enhance your piece. Make sure the piece is clean and free of all dust before beginning.

MATERIALS

METAL LEAF ADHESIVE

PAINTBRUSHES: small craft brush
    for adhesive, soft bristle brush for
    smoothing, and Purdy White China
    Brush Series brush for finishing

METAL LEAF, gold or silver

SANDING SPONGE, fine grit

MINWAX SPECIAL WALNUT STAIN

SHOP TOWELS

continued . . .

TIP ▶ Metal leaf on furniture works great to accent detailed insets, trim, or you can tape off designs like I did on this piece. A little goes a long way, so choose wisely!

TIP ▶ On this piece, I decided to add a metal leaf stripe on the top just for fun! To get this same look, tape off your stripe just like the striping technique on page 78, and follow the metal leafing instructions laid out for you here. Just be sure to stay inside the lines of your tape, and remove your tape immediately when finished metal leafing. Be sure to remove the tape slowly for that perfectly straight edge.

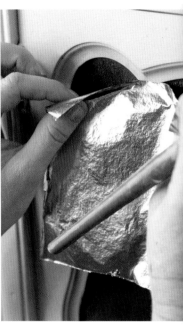

1 ▶ **APPLY THE ADHESIVE** with the small craft paintbrush only to those areas of the furniture where you want to place the metal leaf. The adhesive is very watery, so apply it sparingly, and smooth out any bubbles or liquid puddles so that the application is even and smooth. Be very careful to only put the adhesive exactly where you will be putting the metal leaf, as it dries very sticky. Metal leaf will only stick where the adhesive has been applied.

FIG. A

2 ▶ **ALLOW THE ADHESIVE 1 HOUR** of drying time before applying the metal leaf. This allows the adhesive to "set up" and become tacky.

3 ▶ **ONCE THE ADHESIVE IS SET,** pick up a sheet of metal leaf with your hands and start applying it one sheet at a time, overlapping them just a bit so there are no division lines. Once the metal leaf touches the surface, there is no turning back, so make sure you have it exactly where you want it. You can use the whole sheet at one time, or break the sheet into the size you need. However, the metal leaf tends to break naturally, so it is easiest to just apply the entire sheet. Metal leaf sheets are very delicate and thin, so use care when picking them up as they tear easily.

FIG. B

4 ▶

·········
FIGS. C

SMOOTH THE METAL LEAF using your fingers and/or the soft-bristle brush. Gently brush away any excess metal leaf. It is pretty forgiving, so if you have a couple of wrinkles or bare spots, just smooth them out with the brush, and add more leafing where it may not have adhered the first time. Continue to apply the metal leaf until the entire area is completely covered.

5 ▶

·········
FIG. D

ONCE COVERED, you can leave it as it is, or you can sand it a little bit with a fine sanding sponge to give it a worn look. Be careful not to sand too much, and use an extremely light touch or you will quickly end up without any metal leaf left on your surface!

6 ▶

·········
FIGS. E

WHEN THE SANDING IS COMPLETE, you will want to seal your metal leaf as soon as possible to avoid it oxidizing, and to protect your beautiful finish. There are specific sealants for leafing, but I love to add a stain (see page 56) over the top of all of my leafing finishes. I personally feel like it adds a depth to the finish that the clear sealants do not, while adding a layer of protection as well. Apply the stain using the China brush over the entire piece of furniture for a uniform look. Use a clean shop towel to wipe and smooth the stain as you go.

APPLYING
MILK PAINT

Milk paint is my favorite paint to work with. Its earthy tones, washed finish, and self-distressing tendencies are perfect for maintaining the integrity of a piece of furniture while also giving it a truly authentic time-worn look. Milk paint is very user friendly, and easy to apply. Before you start, prep the furniture piece by lightly sanding with a fine to medium sanding sponge (see page 36) and then clean the surface with a clean damp shop towel. Fill any old hardware holes that you will not be using with wood filler (see page 40) and drill any new holes. Do not use any type of wood cleaner or solvent, as it will leave an oily film on the surface and may seep through the paint or prevent the paint from adhering properly.

MATERIALS

MEASURING CUP, for measuring and mixing (see tip)

MILK PAINT POWDER

HOT WATER

STIR STICK

PAINTBRUSHES: Purdy Nylox brush for paint and White China Brush Series brush for finish

SANDING SPONGES, fine and medium grits

VACUUM

ORBITAL SANDER (optional)

SHOP TOWELS

POLYURETHANE, water or oil based

PAPER FOR DRAWERS (optional)

TIP ▶ Mixing milk paint is almost as important as the application! I use plastic measuring cups from Home Depot for both measuring and mixing milk paint. Milk paint comes in both premixed and powder form, but I personally prefer the powder. It is really easy to mix.

TIP ▶ One really important thing to remember is that as milk paint dries, it is completely porous and unprotected. You will want to keep any oils, moisture, and solvents away from the surface until you have properly sealed it.

1 ▶ **TO MIX THE MILK PAINT,** use the measuring cup to mix equal parts powder and water. Hot water works best for mixing, and when I say mixing, I mean lots of mixing! Mix with a paint stirring stick until all of the lumps are gone and the paint is nice and smooth. I suggest mixing every now and again throughout the project to make sure the paint stays smooth.

2 ▶ **APPLY THE PAINT** with a Nylox brush, in the direction of the wood grain. Be careful not to overwork the paint with excessive brushing back and forth, and apply in nice long, even strokes. I love to use a brush application because it gives the paint finish more depth. Milk paint can sometimes seem a little translucent when applying the first coat, but once the first coat has dried and the second coat is applied, your surface will be covered completely. As milk paint dries, it starts to look very chalky and it flakes and lifts off the piece of furniture where it does not want to adhere. This can be a scary moment, but it is exactly what is supposed to happen. Experiment with the level of coverage that best suits the piece you are creating.

....
FIGS. A

continued . . .

3

FIG. B

AFTER THE FIRST COAT OF PAINT is completely dry, lightly sand with a fine sanding sponge to remove any loose or flaking paint. If you skip this step, you may end up with a lumpy texture in your finish. Using a vacuum, go over the entire surface to remove all sanding dust.

4

WHEN YOU HAVE FINISHED SANDING, apply the second coat of paint. Milk paint dries within 1 to 1½ hours, so you do not have to wait long in between coats.

5

FIG. C

WHEN THE PIECE IS COMPLETELY DRY, it is time to sand again. This sanding is to remove any lingering paint flakes, but also to create the texture pattern that you would like for the piece. You can choose to hand sand here with a fine sanding sponge for a more natural look, or you can use an orbital sander to create a highly distressed look. Milk paint tends to be a self-distressing paint, and will do most of the initial work for you. The most important thing to remember here is to remove all loose paint, because you do not want it flaking off after the final polyurethane finish has been applied. Vacuum, and wipe down with a shop towel after sanding to remove all dust.

6

FIG. D

APPLY THE FIRST COAT OF POLYURE-THANE with a China brush, and let it dry for 2 hours before sanding with a fine sanding sponge. After lightly sanding down the entire piece, vacuum and wipe down with a clean shop towel to remove all sanding dust before applying the second coat. If you are using your milk paint piece as a sink fixture or any other surface that will get lots of wear and tear, I highly recommend an oil-based polyurethane for proper water protection.

7

ATTACH THE NEW HARDWARE (see page 44), and, if using, line the drawers with paper (see page 118).

B

C

D

USING
VINYL DECALS

Vinyl decals are basically just big stickers! They come in many shapes and sizes and can be applied to walls, furniture, doors, and windows. You can purchase them from multiple online sites, but I ordered this particular arrow pattern on Etsy.com. Vinyl decals are an easy way to add eye-catching detail to a piece of furniture and can be done one of two ways: You can use a painted piece, and apply vinyl as a topcoat design that remains on the surface, or you can use the vinyl as a reverse technique. I chose the reverse technique here for my design. I love to apply vinyl decals, paint over them, and then let the natural wood shine through once the vinyl has been peeled off.

MATERIALS

SANDING SPONGE, fine grit

VACUUM

SHOP TOWELS

VINYL DECAL

SCISSORS

YELLOW FROGTAPE

PLASTIC SQUEEGEE

PAINT

PAINT TRAY

PAINTBRUSHES: Purdy Nylox brush
    for painting and White China
    Brush Series brush for finish

FOAM ROLLER

POLYURETHANE, water based

TIP I have seen some beautiful decal designs with large masted ships, maps of the world, sea creatures, and long quotes. It really depends on your level of comfort as to how detailed your design plan is, but the actual application is the same no matter what type or size of decal design you choose. Here, I chose a modern arrow pattern that I felt complemented the design of this mid-century piece.

TIP Before you start, plan out where you want to place the vinyl on the piece of furniture and make sure that the decal fits in the area you have chosen. If you want to put half the design on the side of the piece and then have it carry onto the top (as I did with the arrows in this technique), go ahead and figure that out.

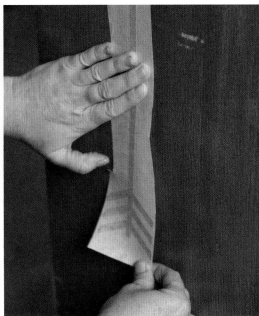

1 ▶ **LIGHTLY SAND DOWN** the entire furniture piece with a fine sanding sponge (see page 36). Be sure to give extra attention to the areas of wood that will have the vinyl over them, as they need to be perfectly smooth. If you are choosing to do the reverse technique described here, you will want the wood surface that will show to be even and smooth, not blotchy and scarred. When the sanding is complete, remove all the dirt and sanding dust with a vacuum and then wipe the surface down with a shop towel.

2 ▶ **IF THERE ARE SEVERAL PIECES** to the vinyl
....
FIG. A decal, cut out each one with scissors so that it is easier to get the placement perfect. When you are ready to begin applying the vinyl, place a piece of FrogTape over your vinyl piece at the halfway point. This is to keep the vinyl decal in place, and to help you apply the decal smoothly, one half at a time. Taping is a must, and will ensure the smoothest application.

3 ▶ **REMOVE THE BACKING OF YOUR VINYL**
....
FIGS. B up to the piece of tape at the halfway point. Carefully cut the backing off. Make sure to keep the sticky part of the vinyl off the surface of the furniture until you are ready to press it down.

4 ▶ **START PRESSING THE DESIGN DOWN,**
....
FIG. C beginning at the top and working downward and out. Make sure your placement is right the first time; once the vinyl is on the surface, it can't be removed without damaging the decal.

5 ▶ **ONCE YOU GET THE FIRST HALF DOWN,** remove the tape and peel away the backing from the other half of the design. Press down the rest of the design as described.

6 ▶ **THE SQUEEGEE TOOL** that comes with most
....
FIGS. D
(PAGE 78) vinyl decal purchases is essential. Once you have placed the sticky side onto the piece of furniture, very gently but firmly run the squeegee back and forth from side to side over the

continued . . .

entire design. This removes all air bubbles that may have become trapped during application, and transfers the vinyl securely to the surface of the furniture. When you are sure that your vinyl has transferred completely, very gently begin to peel away the top layer of paper. You will want to do this slowly and carefully in case you may have missed a spot and need to go back and apply more pressure.

7 ▶ **ONCE ALL OF THE VINYL HAS BEEN APPLIED** to the piece of furniture, it is time to start painting over the decals. Pour the paint into the paint tray and paint the entire surface of the furniture in the color of your choice (see page 52). I chose a nice gray here to complement the wood tone of my piece. I recommend using a foam roller, because it distributes the right amount of paint without getting too thick around the vinyl, but a Nylox brush can also be used. Light coats are required here!

FIG. E

8 ▶ **PAINT ONE COAT,** and allow it to dry according to the manufacturer's instructions (typically 1 to 2 hours). Then apply the second coat of paint exactly as you applied the first.

9 ▶ **AFTER THE SECOND COAT HAS DRIED** to the touch, go ahead and remove the vinyl. Be careful when getting the first corner of your vinyl pieces started—do not chip or scratch your painted surface. I find that removing it slowly, with both hands and with even tension, is the best way to ensure a smooth removal.

FIG. F

10 ▶ **ONCE ALL OF THE VINYL HAS BEEN REMOVED,** it is time to apply a protective finish. I chose a clear water-based polyurethane, applied with a China brush, in order to give this design the protection it needs to stand up to wear and tear. Apply two to three coats of polyurethane, with proper drying time and light sanding between each coat (see page 48).

USING
STENCILS

Stencils provide wonderful creative opportunities for those of us who may not be gifted in the freehand drawing department! It is relatively simple to incorporate gorgeous design elements using stencils, and the results can be stunning. Sometimes just a few intentionally placed circles make the perfect finish. I am a big fan of the stencils and books by Ed Roth of Stencil1. The design featured here is from his book *Stencil 101*. Before you start, plan out your design. It is really important to know exactly where your stencils will go in order to get the final design you want.

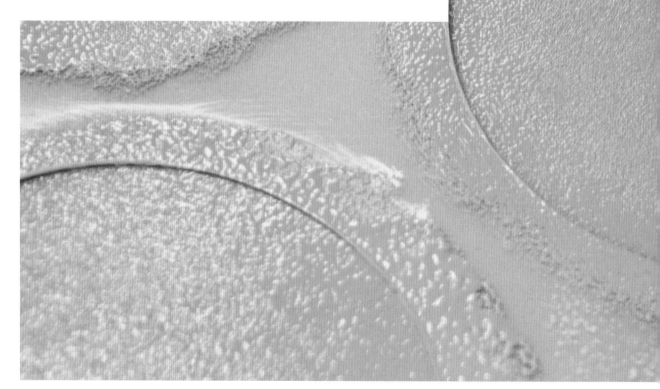

MATERIALS

STENCIL

PENCIL

YELLOW FROGTAPE

SPONGE BRUSH

PAINT, satin finish latex

SHOP TOWELS

SANDING SPONGE, fine grit

PLASTIC GLOVES

STAIN

PAINTBRUSH, Purdy White China
   Brush series

TIP ▶ You can use your stencil to
draw out the entire design
with a pencil first and go
back and fill in the design
by hand. This method is a
bit more labor intensive
than the one I use for this
project.

continued . . .

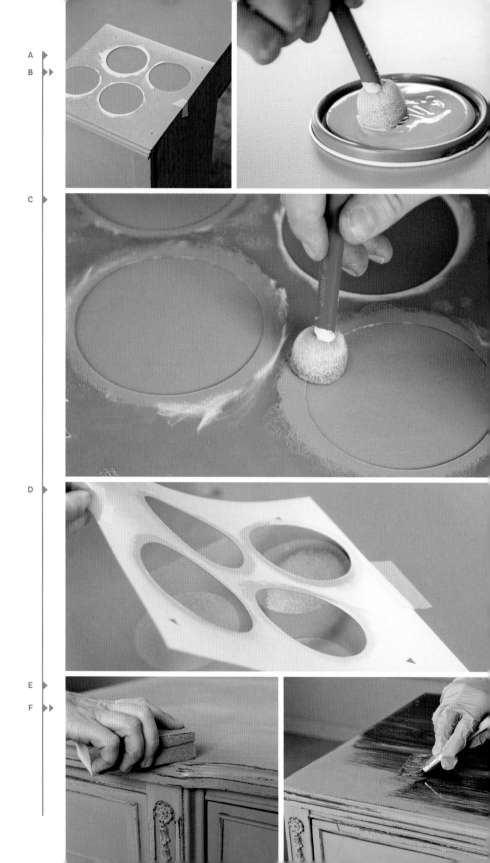

1 ▶ **TO LAY OUT THE DESIGN,** place the stencils where you want them and use a pencil to lightly mark where the corners of the stencils should go. You'll follow these marks to lay down the stencils when you start designing.

2 ▶ **ONCE THE DESIGN PLAN IS LAID OUT,** go ahead and place the first stencil. Use a couple of pieces of FrogTape to secure the stencil.

FIG. A

3 ▶ **DIP YOUR SPONGE BRUSH** in the paint and dab it on a shop towel to remove excess paint. In stenciling, less is more! It is better to do a couple of light coats than to have too much paint on your brush and end up with bleeding paint lines in your design.

FIG. B

4 ▶ **GENTLY APPLY THE PAINT** to the stenciled area with a dabbing motion. Use light pressure so the paint will be nice and smooth. Repeat this until you have filled in the entire stencil.

FIG. C

5 ▶ **WHEN DOING A REPEAT PATTERN,** immediately remove the stencil, wipe it clean, and place it in the next position. Repeat this process until the entire design is complete.

FIG. D

6 ▶ **WHEN THE FIRST COAT IS DRY** to the touch, go back and place the stencil where you first started and apply the second coat.

7 ▶ **AFTER THE STENCILED DESIGN IS COMPLETE,** let it dry completely for 2 to 4 hours, and then lightly sand over the top with a fine sanding sponge. I like to do this in order to get rid of any raised edges and give the stenciled designs a nice "washed" appearance. Wipe it down with a clean shop towel to remove all sanding dust.

FIG. E

8 ▶ **WEARING GLOVES, APPLY PROTECTIVE COATING** to the surface of the entire piece. I love to use stain because it adds a rich brown age to the paint, while at the same time providing a protective finish. If you decide to apply a water-based polyurethane, you can use the same China brush, since it is designed for both stains and polyurethanes.

FIG. F

USING AN
OVERHEAD PROJECTOR

Using an overhead projector is the perfect way to add detailed designs to your furniture pieces, especially for those of us who may not be the greatest at freehand drawing. The best part is that everything is done for you, and you just have to paint inside the lines! I use this technique when I want to do an oversized design that cannot be achieved with stencils. The great thing about these designs is that they are a little bit more freehand and organic looking than stencils or decals. Paint a base coat on your piece of furniture, so that you have a solid base to trace your design on.

MATERIALS

TRANSPARENCY DESIGN (see tip)

OVERHEAD PROJECTOR (see tip)

PENCIL

RULER

PAINT

PAINTBRUSHES: small flat and angled brushes for painting and Purdy White China Brush Series brush for finish

SANDING SPONGE

VACUUM

SHOP TOWELS

POLYURETHANE

TIP ▶ Packs of transparency paper can be expensive, but for just a few cents you can e-mail your design to Kinko's FedEx Office (formally) or OfficeMax and they will print it for you.

TIP ▶ Schools, churches, and used office supply retailers are great places to find overhead projectors, and they are usually very inexpensive. If you can't find an overhead projector, an opaque projector is widely available at art supply stores and will do the exact same thing.

TIP ▶ There are many places you can look online for free art, but a better option is to use software like Adobe Illustrator or Photoshop to create your own custom design. If you do not have the computer skills to work with the software, enlist the help of a designer who can create it for you. Be sure the design will fit within the parameters of your piece. I find that a flat front or tabletop piece works best for this technique.

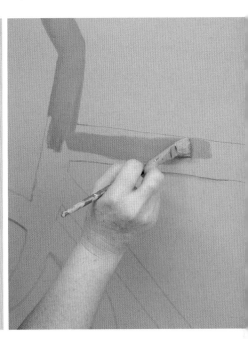

1 ▶ **PRINT YOUR CHOSEN DESIGN** on a transparency.

2 ▶ **ARRANGE THE FURNITURE** so that it is at a good level for you to stand or sit to trace the design. For this table, I elevated it on two platforms so that it would be level and easy for me to trace.

3 ▶ **SET UP YOUR PROJECTOR** and place the transparency on the screen. I typically place my projector on a chair because it is easy to move if needed. Move the projector backward or forward until the design is exactly where you want it on your piece. Adjust the knobs on the projector for size and clarity as well.

....
FIG. A

4 ▶ **WHEN THE DESIGN IS WHERE YOU WANT IT,** begin tracing your design with a pencil. If the design you are tracing has a lot of straight lines, you can use a ruler to make your lines

....
FIG. B

nice and straight. This bike design is one that I chose to leave a little "looser" so I was a bit freeform in my tracing. Just make sure that your lines are dark enough for you to see, but not too dark in case you need to erase and adjust them a bit. To check your lines, walk back to the projector and shut it off. This will allow you to see what you have drawn so far, and make adjustments if needed. As a general rule, though, keep the projector and transparency in the same place throughout the entire tracing process to ensure an even design.

5 ▶ **BEGIN PAINTING,** once the design is completely drawn. I like to use small paintbrushes in both flat and angled shapes for the best accuracy. I always paint just outside of my drawn lines so that they do not show in the end design. Feel free to be creative here and make your design unique.

....
FIG. C

continued . . .

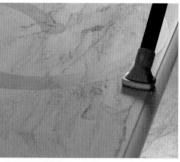

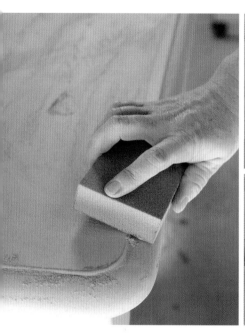

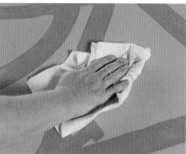

6 ▶ **ALLOW THE FIRST COAT TO DRY** completely (1 to 2 hours) before applying the second coat. The second coat goes much faster as the hard work of applying clean lines is already behind you. You may be able to get the design painted in just one coat depending on the design, but it usually takes two coats to get it where it needs to be.

7 ▶ **WHEN THE PAINTING** of your design is finished and you have allowed it to dry, you can begin sanding with a sanding sponge (see page 36). The level of sanding is completely up to you. You can go for a high level of distressing, light distressing, or you can decide not to distress at all. If you choose not to distress, you can skip the sanding step. It really depends on the design you are working on and the style you are trying to convey. If you sand your piece, vacuum the entire piece with a brush attachment and wipe it down with a clean shop towel to remove all sanding dust.

FIGS. D

8 ▶ **USING THE CHINA BRUSH,** apply a protective finish to ensure that all of your hard work stays fresh. For most pieces, a water-based polyurethane works fine. However, if the piece you choose is a tabletop or a piece to be used in a high-traffic area (like an entryway or den), I highly recommend an oil-based polyurethane finish for long-lasting results (see page 48).

FIG. E

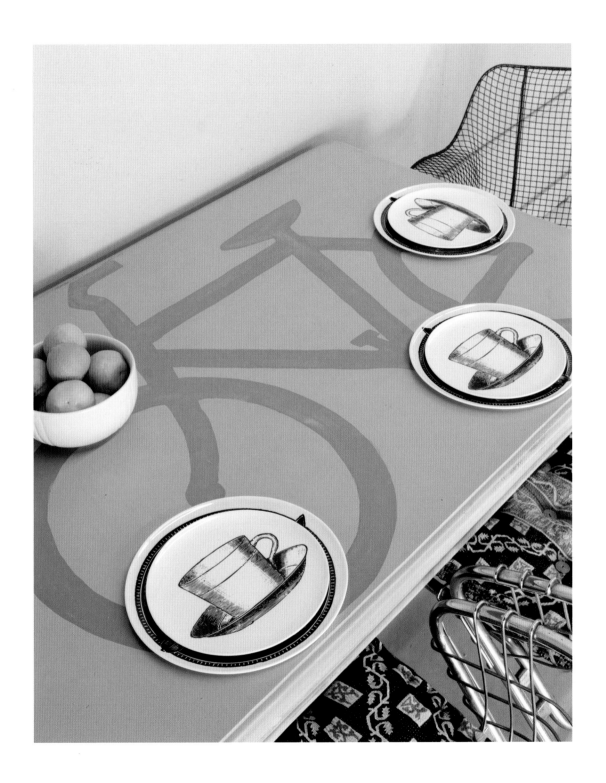

USING
DÉCOUPAGE

Découpage is an age-old technique that was used centuries ago in places like France, China, and Russia and was extremely popular in the 1960s when crafting became the "groovy" thing to do! The word *découpage* actually means "the art of using cut-out paper, plastic, or other flat material over which varnish or lacquer is applied." Over the past several years, découpage has evolved, and even modern enthusiasts have embraced its beauty. Before you start, prepare your piece of furniture by filling any unevenness or holes with wood filler using a putty spatula (see page 40), sanding with a fine sanding sponge (see page 36), and cleaning the surface with a damp shop towel. You want the surface to be completely smooth before you apply the paper design.

MATERIALS

RULER

PAPER FOR YOUR DESIGN (see tip)

SCISSORS OR CRAFT KNIFE

ADHESIVE: wallpaper paste if using wallpaper, or Mod Podge depending on the paper being used

SMALL PAINT TRAY

PAINTBRUSHES: small craft brush for adhesive, Purdy Nylox brush for final Mod Podge layer, and White China Brush Series brush for polyurethane finish

CRAFT KNIFE

PLASTIC SQUEEGEE

MOD PODGE

POLYURETHANE, water based

SANDING SPONGE

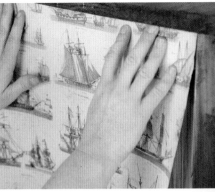

TIP ▶ When I was planning out the design for these two découpage pieces, I really liked the look of newsprint because it appears seamless when cut and layered. However, I wanted something with a bit more design appeal, so I chose a paper that had a small repeating masted ship pattern. When choosing papers for découpage, small tight repeat patterns are great for a nice uniform look. I chose to cover the entire piece of furniture in this technique, but you can also use individual cutouts on specific sections of the piece as well.

TIP ▶ There are so many options for papers, you can use vintage and found papers, wallpaper, newspaper, or wrapping paper. Whichever paper you decide to use, make sure that you have enough to complete your project before you get started. It is always best to plan for a little extra; if you have leftovers you can use it on another project, or use it to line drawers.

1 ▶

....

FIGS. A

MEASURE WITH A RULER and cut the paper carefully with your scissors or craft knife so that it matches the size of the area to be covered. Pour an ample amount of adhesive into a small paint tray, and using the craft brush, apply a thin layer of adhesive to both the surface of the furniture and the back of the paper. You will want to keep the adhesive only in the area where you are working. Adhesive dries quickly, so apply the paper immediately, and lay the paper design down carefully.

2 ▶

....

FIGS. B

ONCE YOU'VE APPLIED THE PAPER to the piece of furniture, smooth it gently with your fingers. I recommend using a small plastic squeegee to get the paper ultra smooth and squeeze out any excess glue that will cause rippling. The most important thing is to work from the center of the paper out to the edges; this technique works out any air bubbles and excess glue. Be sure to keep some extra towels on hand to keep your fingers clean while working with the paper. You do not want to transfer

continued . . .

glue or dirt from your hands to the top of the paper. I promise there will be lots of glue on your fingers, as this is a very messy technique, so try to keep your hands as clean as possible throughout the project.

3 ▶

FIG. C

CONTINUE APPLYING PIECES of paper as stated above, working in sections until the furniture you are working on is entirely covered with the desired amount of paper. Upon completion of each section, apply a layer of Mod Podge over the top with the Nylox brush, especially in a collage design, to ensure proper adhesion.

4 ▶

FIG. D

WHEN ALL OF THE PAPER has been applied, and the Mod Podge is completely dry, it is time to apply a coat of polyurethane to the project. This provides both a nice finished look and protection for the paper you have so lovingly applied to your piece. I highly recommend a polyurethane coating over Mod Podge, because I have found that sometimes Mod Podge can remain "tacky" even when it is completely dry. A polyurethane coat, applied with the China brush, ensures a smoother surface, and will dry completely. After you have applied two to three coats of polyurethane, allowed proper drying times, and sanded lightly with a sanding sponge between each coat, your piece is ready to go.

COLOR BLOCKING

This technique is a very simple way of using one color in several shades to create a beautiful statement piece. Color blocking can be applied with muted tones or bright and colorful tones—it really depends on the style of the room in which it will go. Color blocking works well for nurseries, but can be sophisticated and modern enough for any room in your home. You can go whimsical or classical simply by changing up the color palette and paint application, so be creative based on your personal style. For this technique, I chose a dresser because the drawers naturally lend themselves to a color gradient, but color blocking can be done on several different types of furniture—I've done this for tables, headboards, chairs, and even floors. Before you start, make sure that the piece of furniture you have chosen is completely sanded, cleaned, and ready to paint (see page 36). If you will be using new hardware, be sure to wood fill any holes that will not be used in the new design (see page 40).

MATERIALS

GREEN FROGTAPE

PAINT

PAINT TRAYS, one for each color

PAINTBRUSH: Purdy Nylox brushes for paint (one brush for each color) and White China Brush Series brush for finish

FOAM ROLLERS, for applying the paint to the flat surfaces of the drawers and chest

SANDING SPONGE, fine grit

VACUUM

SHOP TOWELS

POLYURETHANE, water based

PAPER FOR DRAWERS

continued . . .

1 ▶ **TAPE OFF ALL THE EDGES** of any drawers and runners so that you do not get paint on them. You want to keep all of your lines clean and professional.

2 ▶ **POUR EACH PAINT** into a separate tray. Using a Nylox brush to cut in around the edges, and a roller to cover the large flat surfaces, paint the entire base (or background) of the piece in the lightest color of the palette you have chosen. Once the base is painted, start with the front of the very bottom drawer (or at the bottom of whatever piece you choose to color block). It is best to work from the darkest color at the bottom to the lightest color at the top for a nice graduated color effect. Start painting with the darkest color in your palette.

FIG. A

3 ▶ **GO TO THE NEXT DRAWER** or section up and paint the next color in your palette, going from darkest to lightest until you have finished with the top drawer or section.

FIGS. B

4 ▶ **IF YOU CHOOSE TO DISTRESS** the finish of the piece, go ahead and lightly sand the edges with a fine sanding sponge. Make sure all sanding dust is removed from the surface by vacuuming and wiping everything down with a shop towel.

FIG. C

TIP ▶ When choosing your paint colors, I recommend using a paint card that features a gradient of colors to guide you in your decision. Once you have narrowed it down to a specific color, you can pick four or five of your favorites from the same palette.

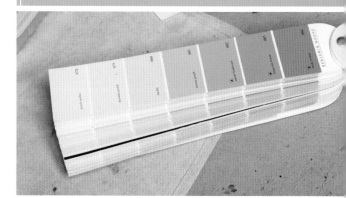

A ▶

APPLY A COAT OF WATER-BASED polyurethane to the entire piece using the China brush. Drying times will vary depending on the product you use, but most water-based polyurethanes will dry within 2 hours. After the first coat is dry, lightly sand the piece, vacuum to remove all sanding dust, wipe down with a clean shop towel, and then apply a second coat.

6

ATTACH HARDWARE AND LINE THE DRAWERS with paper (see page 118) to complete your project. The drawer paper should complement the color and design on the piece. One of the first things people do when looking at a piece of furniture is open the drawers to look inside. Make sure that first impression is a beautiful one!

C

D

ADDING
STRIPES

Stripes are a fun and simple way to add a whimsical or modern touch to furniture, depending on the design and stripe layout that you choose. Sometimes it only takes three or four stripes to complete a piece, and other times it may take twenty, but regardless of how many, the important things to remember are to use the right tape, and make sure your lines are super straight! The mapping out process is an important step, so be sure to take the time to plan it out, and make it intentional.

MATERIALS

MEASURING TAPE OR RULER

PENCIL

FROGTAPE (see tip)

CRAFT KNIFE

PAINT

PAINT TRAY

FOAM ROLLER

PAINTBRUSHES: Purdy Nylox brush for paint and White China Brush Series brush for finish

STAIN OR POLYURETHANE

SANDING SPONGE, fine grit

SHOP TOWELS

PLASTIC GLOVES

continued . . .

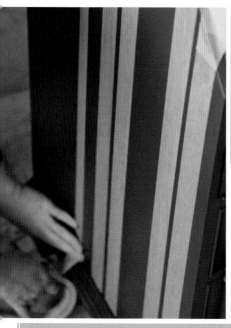

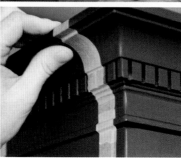

TIP ▶ If you are taping off a piece on which you have recently put a base coat, you will want to use the yellow FrogTape, as it is not quite as sticky as the green and will not damage the new finish. Press the tape firmly when you apply it to prevent any paint from sneaking under the edges. If you decide to have the natural wood become the stripe for the piece, use the green FrogTape, still making sure that the tape is pressed nice and flat. This is key to successful, clean stripes.

1 ▶ **MAP OUT YOUR STRIPES.** For uniform stripes, measure out the entire piece first with measuring tape or a ruler, and mark where each stripe will begin with a pencil. Then use the ruler to lightly pencil in where you will tape off the lines. Be sure that the stripes are evenly distributed on the entire piece before starting to tape. This will save you lots of time and frustration! For an asymmetrical or whimsical striped pattern, just place the tape where you want it on the piece. Think free-hand design!

2 ▶ **BEGIN TAPING OFF YOUR PIECE.** Tear off the piece of tape that you have unrolled and simultaneously adhere the top and the bottom at the same time. Then, press down the rest of the tape line, making sure it is nice and straight. If your tape line is crooked, remove it from the bottom until you reach the area where it started to go wrong and work your way back down. Once you are sure that the tape line is perfectly straight, press very firmly on the entire piece of tape to make sure it is secure.

....
FIG. A

3 ▶

USE YOUR CRAFT KNIFE AND A RULER to trim the tape off at the edges if needed. Sometimes, depending on the shape of the piece and the design plan, you can wrap the tape around the edges and not have to trim it. However, if the design plan has specific cutoff points, the lines must be perfectly straight and neat in order to get the desired effect.

4 ▶
FIG. C

POUR PAINT INTO A TRAY and begin painting. A foam roller will give you the thinnest and smoothest layer of paint, but sometimes the width of the stripes may not allow for a roller and you will need to use a brush. It is totally okay to use either, but remember to use light coats of paint so that you do not get buildup at the tape line. You want the stripes to appear seamless. If there is any thick buildup it will tend to peel when you lift up the tape and cause a very messy stripe. The goal is perfect lines!

5 ▶

DO NOT REMOVE THE TAPE until you are completely done with the striping pattern, as it will be hard to get it back in the same place, but do remove it as soon as you are done for the best results. Remove the tape while the paint is still wet; it is super important to remove the tape immediately when finished!

6 ▶
FIGS. D

ONCE THE PAINT HAS COMPLETELY DRIED, you can leave the surface as it is and move on to either a stain or polyurethane finish using a China brush, or you can sand and weather your piece using a fine sanding sponge before applying the finish. (For this piece, I sanded the entire piece down [see Sanding Furniture, page 36] and then applied Minwax Special Walnut stain for a polished depth [see Staining Over Paint, page 56].) Wear gloves when you apply the stain.

ACHIEVING THE
DIP-DYED LOOK

The dip-dye technique may be a bit trendy in the furniture world, but if done correctly, the look can be timeless. I love when a little of the original finish shows through in designs, and the dip-dye technique is the perfect opportunity to let this happen. I always choose pieces of furniture for this look that have long narrow legs, like side tables, desks, and chairs. The long, turned legs lend themselves to the dip-dyed effect, and prove to be the most dramatic in appearance. In order to get the look I wanted for the piece pictured for this technique, I stripped and sanded the legs first to make them a little bit lighter. I only stripped the legs, because I wanted there to be more contrast between the wooden legs and the paint color that I chose. You can choose to strip the entire piece, but in this design plan, only the legs need to be stripped (see Stripping Furniture, page 32 and Sanding Furniture, page 36.)

MATERIALS

MEASURING TAPE

PENCIL

GREEN FROGTAPE

PAINT

PAINT TRAY

PAINTBRUSHES: Purdy Nylox
  brush for paint and White China
  Brush Series brush for finish

FOAM ROLLER

SANDING SPONGE, fine grit

SHOP TOWELS

POLYURETHANE, satin water based

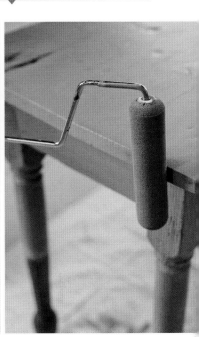

TIP ▶ There are many different ways to dip-dye furniture. In this case, I used a small farm table, but you can also dip-dye desks, chairs, hardware, and chests of drawers. I chose to leave the legs natural wood, but you could paint the legs in a different color, too.

1 ▶   **DECIDE HOW MUCH** of the leg you want to remain natural wood and measure and mark it with a pencil where you will need to apply the FrogTape. Sometimes a leg will have a defini-tive marking that makes the taping job easy, such as a break in the turn of the leg design or a definite cutoff point.

....
FIG. A

2 ▶   **APPLY THE TAPE** exactly where you have decided you want your paint line to start. On a round leg this can be tricky. It is hard to get the tape perfect all the way around, and you may have to adjust it a couple of times to make sure it is right. It is important that the tape is perfect, so that your line will be perfect, and the final piece will have that great dip-dyed look.

....
FIG. B

continued . . .

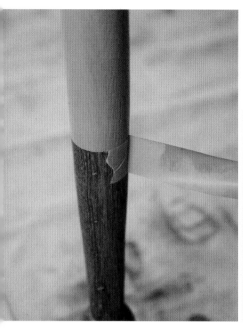  

3 ▶

FIGS. C
(PAGE 101)

POUR SOME PAINT into a tray and paint everything above the tape line. Be very careful not to get any paint below the tape line! You can use a Nylox brush or a foam roller, but be sure to distribute the paint evenly and sparingly. Allow the first coat to dry for about 1 hour, and then apply a second coat.

4 ▶

FIG. D

ONCE THE SECOND COAT has been applied, remove the tape and allow the second coat to dry completely.

5 ▶

FIG. E

USING A FINE SANDING SPONGE, sand the piece around the edges for some light distressing, but be careful not to sand around the dip-dyed lines. You will want to keep those lines nice and crisp. Wipe it down with a clean shop towel to remove all sanding dust.

6 ▶

FIG. F

USING THE CHINA BRUSH, apply two to three coats of the polyurethane over the entire piece. Follow the manufacturer's drying times and sanding instructions for applying multiple polyurethane coats. This will give the natural wood a nice finished shine, and provide protection for the entire finished surface.

DRY BRUSHING

Dry brushing is a technique that allows you to get a very textured and washed look with very little paint. The end result is an aged wood or driftwood appearance that is absolutely beautiful. It gives the look of pickled or whitewashed wood without all the added steps. It is one of those techniques that looks difficult, but is simple to achieve.

MATERIALS

ORBITAL SANDER

VACCUUM

SHOP TOWELS

PAINT

PAINT TRAY

PAINTBRUSHES: Purdy 2-inch
    Nylox Glide brush for paint,
    and White China Brush Series
    dry paintbrush for blending
    (optional)

SANDING SPONGE, fine grit

POLYURETHANE, oil based (see tip)

 TIP ▶ Because this is a table and may get more than the usual amount of wear and tear, I chose an oil-based polyurethane.

A

1 ▸

FIG. A

LIGHTLY SAND THE ENTIRE PIECE you are getting ready to paint (see page 36). Vacuum and wipe down the entire surface with shop towels to make sure it is free of all dust and dirt before you start your paint application.

2 ▸

B

POUR THE PAINT into a paint tray. Very lightly dip the Nylox brush into the paint until just the very tips of the bristles have a little bit of paint on them. When I say lightly dip, I mean *barely* put the tips of the brush in the paint!

3 ▸

FIG. B

HAVE A FEW FOLDED SHOP TOWELS on hand, so you can dab your paintbrush before applying it to the piece of furniture.

4 ▸

FIGS. C

C

ONCE YOU HAVE DABBED your brush so that the paint is super sparse on the tips of the brush (almost dry to the touch), place it on the surface of the furniture and very quickly move the brush back and forth. Work horizontally on flat surfaces and vertically on all detailed and up and down surfaces. Paint with the grain of wood, covering as much territory as possible before the brush runs out of paint. It is super important (and I mean it!) to keep a light touch here, and work quickly so that your strokes are nice and even. The very first place you touch with the brush is going to be heavier than the other areas, so the best way to even that out is to go back when your brush has run out of paint and very quickly brush back and forth over that area. The secret weapon for this technique is lightning-fast hands. It only took about 25 minutes to paint the first coat on this table. If you feel like you applied paint too heavily in a certain area, use a shop towel or a dry paintbrush and immediately blend the heaviness out. Once the paint dries a bit, you can use a fine sanding sponge to blend as well, but it is best to get it blended as soon as possible.

continued . . .

5 ▶ **CONTINUE TO DIP YOUR NYLOX BRUSH,** dabbing it on a shop towel before application, until the entire piece is covered. If you feel like the paint is getting too heavy, you may need to rinse and dry your brush and start again. I usually rinse my brush out one time during application to make sure that the thickness of the paint remains uniform.

6 ▶ **ONCE THE ENTIRE PIECE** is covered, allow it to dry for 1 hour. The paint should have been applied lightly, so it will not take long to dry.

7 ▶ **ONCE DRY,** lightly sand down the entire piece with a fine sanding sponge, paying special attention to any areas where you feel like you may have slowed up and applied the paint too heavily. You will not need to apply much pressure with the sanding sponge. Wipe it down with a clean shop towel to remove all sanding dust.

....

FIG. D

8 ▶ **APPLY TWO TO THREE COATS** of polyurethane with the China brush and allow proper drying time between each coat for your final finish.

....

FIG. E

D ▶

E ▶

LAYERING PAINT

Using more than one color on a furniture piece allows you to be even more creative in your color choices and finishes. Layering colors adds a depth to the piece of furniture that can't be achieved with just one color. The goal with this technique is to achieve the timeworn, "I have painted this piece a million times with several different colors" look. Before you start, make sure the piece of furniture is sanded, cleaned, and ready to accept paint (see page 36).

PAINTS, one base color and one topcoat color in complementary colors (see tip)

PAINT TRAYS, one for each color

PAINTBRUSHES: one Purdy Nylox brush for base color and one for topcoat color, and White China Brush Series brush for finish (if using stain or polyurethane)

FOAM ROLLER

SANDING SPONGE, fine grit

VACUUM

SHOP TOWELS

WAX BRUSH (if using wax)

WAX, STAIN, OR POLYURETHANE

continued . . .

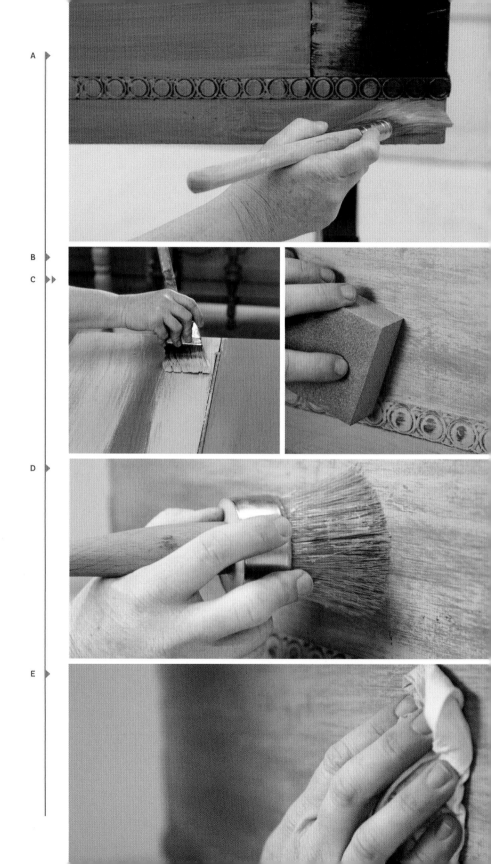

A ▶

B ▶
C ▶▶

D ▶

E ▶

1 ▶ **POUR EACH OF THE PAINT COLORS** into a tray. Apply the base color to the entire surface using a Nylox brush to cut in, and a foam roller for larger flat surfaces. Be sure to cover the entire area evenly and completely.

FIG. A

2 ▶ **ALLOW THE PAINT TO DRY** according to the manufacturer's instructions. I used a product called Chalk Paint for this technique, and it dries very quickly and is usually ready for a second coat within an hour.

3 ▶ **ONCE THE FIRST BASE COAT IS DRY,** apply a second coat. (If you feel like the first coat is solid enough, and you do not need a second coat, you can move on to the topcoat.) Allow the second coat to dry exactly as the first.

4 ▶ **ONCE THE BASE** coat(s) is completely dry, it is time to apply the topcoat. When layering colors, you want to apply the topcoat a little more lightly than the base coat, so that the base coat will show through. Also, you do not want to have to sand through a thick topcoat to get to the base coat.

FIG. B

5 ▶ **ALLOW THE TOPCOAT TO DRY** thoroughly, and begin sanding with a fine sanding sponge. You will have to apply pretty firm pressure to work your way through the top coat of paint. Sand the entire piece, but focus a little more intentionally on the edges and areas where you want the base color to shine through. I chose this particular piece because of the great curves and trim detail that would make this technique shine.

FIG. C

6 ▶ **ONCE THE PIECE IS** completely sanded, vacuum the surface to remove all sanding dust. Use a shop towel after the vacuum to remove any lingering residue.

7 ▶ **TO FINISH THE PAINT** surface, I used a wax brush dipped in clear wax and waxed the entire surface (see page 58). If you choose to use latex paint for this technique, you can still finish with wax or you can choose a stain or polyurethane applied with a China Brush. (If using a stain, wear plastic gloves when applying. I did not wear gloves in this tutorial because I used a clear wax, but feel free to wear gloves to keep your hands wax-free.)

FIG. D

8 ▶ **WAX DRIES IN MINUTES,** so you can quickly begin buffing with a towel in order to bring out the wonderful sheen that a wax finish gives.

FIG. E

TIP ▶ There really is no limit to the combination of colors you can use for this technique, but some of my favorite duos are light gray and orange, turquoise and red, black and red, black over white, light blue and slate blue, and any gray combination! As far as which color to layer where? I say that if the colors are about the same level of pigment, you can do it either way. But, if you have two colors that vary greatly in tone, the technique works best with the lighter color on top and the darker color underneath. I used two colors for this technique, but you can use up to four colors successfully.

SPRAY PAINTING

Spray painting is great for small projects like mirrors, side tables, stools, and chairs. There is a wide variety of beautiful colors to choose from, and when applied correctly, spray paint leaves a perfectly smooth finish. I will only use Krylon and Montana Gold brand spray paints because Krylon has a great fan nozzle that sprays more evenly than other spray paints and Montana Gold is a matte, highly pigmented paint that comes in brilliant colors. Krylon is available at most hardware and craft stores, while Montana Gold is available online and at local art supply stores.

MATERIALS

SANDING SPONGE, fine

DROP CLOTHS

GREEN FROGTAPE

RESPIRATOR (see page 25)

SAFETY GLASSES

SPRAY PAINT

KRYLON CRYSTAL CLEAR SATIN
   FINISH

TIP ▶ Make sure that the area in which you are spray painting is well ventilated, or if the weather is good, paint outside. Spray painting creates a lot of over-spray, so be sure that you cover anything and everything you want to keep clean. You can use drop cloths or plastic for this, but be sure you take the time to do it.

Spray paint has high VOC (volatile organic compound) levels, so it is important to wear a respirator when applying it to keep your lungs safe from the harsh chemicals. I also recommend safety glasses to keep your eyes protected from airborne chemicals and toxins.

1 ▶ **SAND AND PREPARE THE FURNITURE PIECE,** and make sure it is clean and clear of all dust before starting to spray paint (see page 36).

.... FIG. A

2 ▶ **LAY DOWN A DROPCLOTH** underneath your work area. Using the FrogTape, tape off all areas where you do not want overspray. For instance, on this little table, I taped off the corners for a specific design effect, but you can also tape off casters, legs, or other parts of the furniture that will not get painted.

.... FIG. B

3 ▶ **WEARING A RESPIRATOR** and safety glasses, shake the spray paint can vigorously before starting, to make sure it is mixed well. Shake the can every few minutes when painting.

4 ▶ **START SPRAYING YOUR FURNITURE** piece. The key to spray painting is to keep your hand moving! Start the spray off the piece, paint where you want, and end the spray off the piece. This ensures that you will not have the "spotty" spray paint effect. Make sure your strokes are nice and long. Keep the spray stream 10 to

.... FIG. C

11 inches away from the piece while spraying so that you do not end up with too much paint in any given area, and therefore avoid drips.

5 ▶ **WITH SPRAY PAINT,** it is best to do several light coats rather than thick heavy ones. Some spray paints dry in as little as 10 to 12 minutes, so it will not be long before you can apply more coats.

6 ▶ **ONCE YOU ARE SATISFIED** with the level of coverage, it is time to let the piece dry. If you have used tape to tape off a design in your project, as I have done here, now is the time to remove it. Once the piece is completely dry, apply two coats of the clear Krylon topcoat as a finish. Be sure to let each coat dry thoroughly before applying the next coat.

.... FIG. D

Note: With this particular project, I did not do any sanding or distressing before finishing. I chose to leave this table solid and modern looking. Feel free to sand your pieces before applying the clear coat in order to achieve the look you want.

SEAT UPHOLSTERING

It is amazing what a new covering of fabric and a coat of paint will do to transform a piece. While I leave the big upholstery jobs to the professionals, simple chair pads like this one are easy to tackle (I promise!) and can really liven up a space. It's time to flex those DIY muscles, ladies and gents!

MATERIALS

SCREWDRIVERS: One for removing
    screws and a flathead screwdriver
    for removing staples

PLIERS

FABRIC

SCISSORS, fabric cutting

BATTING

STAPLES, ³⁄₈ inch

STAPLE GUN

continued . . .

1 ▶ **FLIP OVER THE CHAIR** and remove the chair pad using a screwdriver to unscrew the four screws holding the pad in place. Keep track of your screws, though, because you will need them again!

FIG. A

2 ▶ **REMOVE THE EXISTING FABRIC** and padding. Sometimes there are several layers of fabric from previous coverings, so be sure to remove all of the layers. To do this properly, use the flathead screwdriver to get underneath and loosen the staples. Usually the staples will come right out when lifted by the screwdriver, but if you have a stubborn staple that wants to stay in the wood, you may need to use pliers to get the staple out completely.

FIGS. B

3 ▶ **IF THE ORIGINAL PIECE OF FABRIC IS STILL IN GOOD SHAPE,** you can use it as a pattern for cutting the new piece. This is the easiest route to go, but if you cannot use the fabric, place the wooden chair pad frame from which you removed all of the fabric onto the reverse

FIG. C

side of your new fabric and, using scissors, cut your new piece. Make sure you leave 2 to 3 inches of excess fabric past the wooden chair pad pattern to ensure that you will have enough fabric to wrap around the edges.

4 ▶ **YOU WILL WANT TO USE NEW BATTING,** if the existing batting is unusable due to wear and tear or if you desire to add more cushion to the seat. Go ahead and cut your new piece. The batting should be the exact same size as the wooden chair pad frame. It should not extend over the edges; you don't want any extra bulk that could cause the seat cushion to sit unevenly on the chair.

5 ▶ **POSITION THE WOODEN CHAIR PAD FRAME** onto the fabric. Make sure the design is where you want it on the pad before starting to staple the fabric in place. For instance, the fabric I chose for this was an ikat design and I wanted to be sure the largest part of the design was in the center of the chair pad.

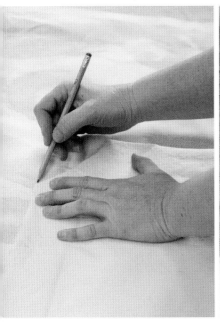
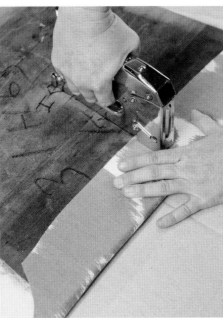

6 ▶ **FOLD OVER THE TOP PIECE** of the fabric and place your first staple directly into the center at the back of the frame for placement. Next, fold over the bottom piece and place a staple in the center at the back of the frame as well. These two staples will serve as your anchors, and will keep everything in place while you start to attach the rest of fabric.

....
FIG. D

7 ▶ **NOW, WORK YOUR WAY AROUND** the entire chair seat, gently pulling the fabric and stapling it to the back of the frame every inch or so. Be careful not to pull your fabric too tightly, as that can distort the pattern and stretch the fabric. It is a good idea to flip the chair pad over and check it every few staples to make sure everything is nice and straight.

8 ▶ **WHEN YOU GET TO THE CORNERS** of the chair, you will want to trim any excess fabric that may cause bulk. Fold the corners neatly by pushing the fabric in with your index finger at the corner point and then folding the two

....
FIG. E

sides smoothly over the top. Place the corner staple back about 1½ inches from the edge of the chair seat so as not to create bulk right where the chair seat attaches to the chair.

9 ▶ **TRIM OFF ANY EXCESS FABRIC.** You want the lines to be as clean and straight as possible, so take care in trimming!

10 ▶ **LOCATE YOUR SCREWS,** place the chair seat into the chair, and screw the screws back in to reattach the chair pad.

LINING DRAWERS

Details matter! I line all of the drawers of my furniture pieces with paper because I feel like it is a finishing detail that should not be overlooked. The papered drawers not only become a part of the design plan that makes opening the drawers a treat, but they also provide a clean and fresh surface for storing all of your belongings.

MATERIALS

VACUUM

WOOD CLEANER

SHOP TOWELS

WALLPAPER OR WRAPPING
    PAPER SHEETS

RULER

PAPER SCISSORS

CRAFT KNIFE

DOUBLE-SIDED MOUNTING TAPE

 TIP ▶ There are times when I will permanently adhere the paper to the insides of the drawers when I want the paper to be a permanent part of the design plan. If I am permanently adhering wallpaper to the inside of the drawer, I use wallpaper paste. If I am using decorative paper sheets, I adhere the paper with Mod Podge and use Benjamin Moore's Ben-wood Stays Clear polyurethane on top for long-lasting results.

1 ▶ **VACUUM OUT ALL OF THE DRAWERS** to remove any dirt that may have collected over time. Once the entire surface has been vacuumed, clean the inside of the drawers with wood cleaner and a damp shop towel. Be careful not to saturate the wood, but rather wipe it down quickly to clean the surface.

B

C

2 ▶ **PLACE THE ROLL OF PAPER** you've chosen beside the drawer, grab the loose edge, and pull the paper over the top of the drawer. This is the easiest way to measure with a ruler the length and width that you will need for lining the drawer.

3 ▶ **USE THE SCISSORS TO CUT** the paper to the outside measurements of the drawer. This will leave a little excess once you place the paper inside the drawer, but that is what you want.

FIG. B

D

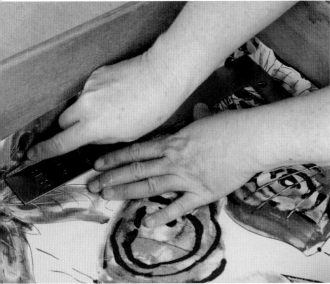

4 ▶ **PLACE THE PAPER INSIDE THE DRAWER,** using the straight uncut edge of the paper as your guide for placement at the front of the drawer. Once that guide is in place, use your fingers to smooth the paper down and crease it into the other three sides of the drawer.

FIG. C

5 ▶ **PLACE THE RULER** up against the edge of the drawer as tight as you can but still leaving room for the craft knife. Keeping the knife to the right (if you are right handed) of the ruler at all times, trim the excess paper. The reason you want to keep the craft knife to the right of the ruler is to ensure a nice straight and even cut every time. The hard edge of the ruler acts as a guide for your craft knife.

FIG. D

E

6 ▶ **ONCE THE PAPER HAS BEEN TRIMMED** to fit the inside of the drawer perfectly, cut four pieces of double-sided mounting tape. Place one piece of tape in each corner of the drawer, and press the paper down onto the tape in order to hold it securely in place.

FIGS. E

BEFORE & AFTER
MAKEOVERS

It is invigorating to take something worn, cast off, and broken and transform it into something fresh, desirable, and beautiful. I never get tired of this process! I love to see what a little sandpaper, paint, and creativity can do to bring new life to a piece of furniture and its surrounding space. I hope to inspire you with these thirty furniture makeovers from my studio, where pieces are given a fresh start and a brand new character. I've highlighted the techniques used on each, so you can replicate the looks at home. Enjoy!

ABELIA

I purchased this piece from a local antique dealer and was instantly drawn to it for its sheer size and the beautiful carved detail. Pieces with this level of detail are harder and harder to come by, so I snatch them up whenever I see them. This piece reminds me of a gentle giant; it just needed a little color to bring it back to life.

BEFORE

1 ▸ Sanded and removed all loose veneer before painting (see Sanding Furniture, page 36)

2 ▸ Tore off the warped backing and replaced it with new oak plywood backing

3 ▸ Painted the piece with milk paints (see Applying Milk Paint, page 72)

LOTTIE

I purchased this piece from the Salvation Army. One of the reasons I picked this lovely lady is because she had flat drawer fronts. They provide multiple design opportunities for both paint and paper applications. I also love any kind of curvy detail, so the curves on the bottom of this piece won me over.

BEFORE

1 ▸ Wood-filled old hardware holes and drilled new holes (see Wood Filling, page 40)

2 ▸ Added bone knobs

3 ▸ Used color blocking to add a graduated color design pattern up the front of the furniture piece (see Color Blocking, page 92)

4 ▸ Applied paint with a foam roller for a super smooth finish (see Painting Furniture, page 52)

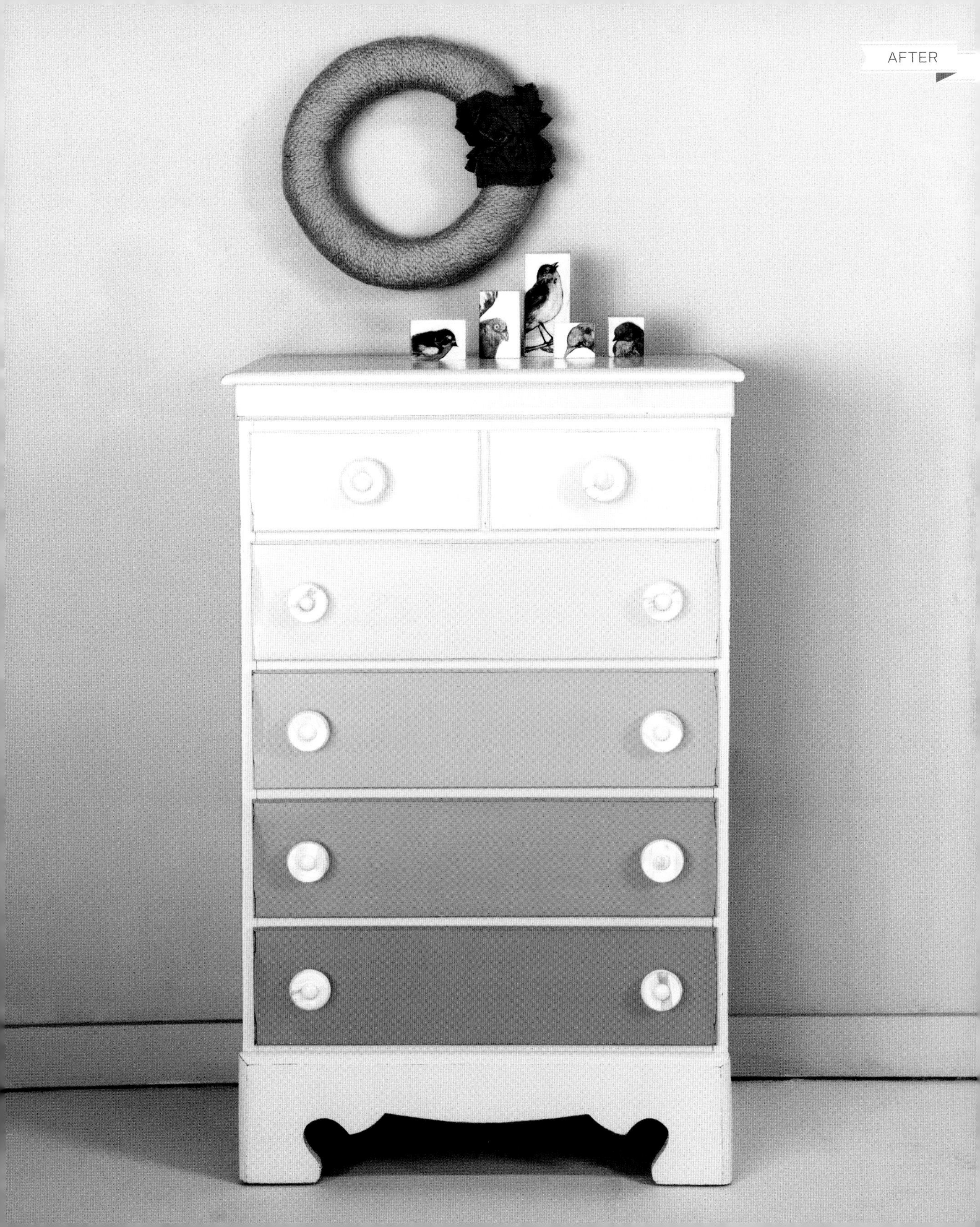

AFTER

ADA

I absolutely love the curved line of this headboard, and the teeny tiny little footboard stood out as a unique detail. I originally thought that I was going to use a wallpaper application on this piece because of the inset design of the headboard; it seemed like a simple way to tie the headboard and footboard together. But I quickly changed my mind and decided to use paint and wax to transform it instead.

BEFORE

1 ▸ Applied turquoise paint with a foam roller (see Painting Furniture, page 52)

2 ▸ Applied brown wax with a wax brush (see Waxing over Paint, page 58)

3 ▸ Sanded over the dry wax with a sanding sponge to blend and smooth

4 ▸ Buffed and polished the wax finish with a rag to get that perfect shine

PRENTICE

This armoire belongs to my parents. Armoires are not used as much these days since most newly constructed homes have giant and abundant closets. But my mom wanted to use this piece for storage on her beautiful new sun porch, and since her favorite color combination is yellow and red, I chose mustard yellow for this piece. You can never go wrong with mustard in my opinion!

BEFORE

1 ▸ Reattached loose insert on the door. Countless nails had to be removed so that the wood would lie flat in the original grooves. I affixed it with wood glue and wood screws for extra stability.

2 ▸ Glued and clamped the cracked door back together (see Gluing & Clamping, page 43)

3 ▸ Applied milk paint (see Applying Milk Paint, page 72)

4 ▸ Attached red glass floral knobs found at Hobby Lobby

MIRROR, MIRROR ON THE WALL

I find that a chest of drawers sells much better when you remove the mirror and sell it as a separate piece. So, I end up with a lot of orphaned mirrors. I chose to paint these as a collection because the multiple styles and colors make a strong artistic statement when hung together. The fact that these particular mirrors had some beautiful detail just made the entire project even more fun.

BEFORE

1 ▸ MUSTARD MIRROR

Removed the wooden attachment frame and wood-filled the side holes.

Applied milk paint with a Nylox paintbrush (see Applying Milk Paint, page 72)

Sanded to remove all loose flakes

Applied a clear wax finish

2 ▸ GRAY MIRROR

Lightly sanded to prep the surface (see Sanding Furniture, page 36)

Applied gray latex paint with a Nylox paintbrush

Sanded and distressed

Applied brown wax finish

3 ▸ GREEN MIRROR

Removed the long attachment pieces from the back of the mirror so that the mirror would have a nice straight line on the bottom

Wood-filled the holes (see Wood Filling, page 40)

Applied Knack custom green paint in latex. (This is a color that I mixed, and have named it Esme Green after the first piece I used it on.) (see Painting Furniture, page 52)

Lightly sanded and finished the surface in a brown wax (see Waxing over Paint, page 58)

4 ▸ TURQUOISE MIRROR

Wood-filled the side holes (see Wood Filling, page 40)

Applied turquoise latex paint with a Nylox brush (see Painting Furniture, page 52)

Sanded and finished the surface with brown wax (see Waxing over Paint, page 58)

Attached hardware for hanging

CALVINA

I purchased this piece from a local antique dealer who had just bought out an estate. While I was gathering other pieces, he pulled out this coffee table and said, "Hey, what about this?" I'm not typically drawn to modern pieces, and I did not like this one at first. I kept staring at it though, and soon a plan began to form in my mind about what I could do to make it fresh and new.

BEFORE

1 ▸ Removed the tray top because I wanted a clean slate

2 ▸ Wood-filled the screw holes (see Wood Filling, page 40)

3 ▸ Measured, taped off, and painted each triangular section (see Adding Stripes, page 96)

4 ▸ Applied water-based polyurethane finish over paint (see Applying Polyurethane, page 48)

5 ▸ Lightly sanded and refreshed the natural wood with Danish oil on the legs and drawer

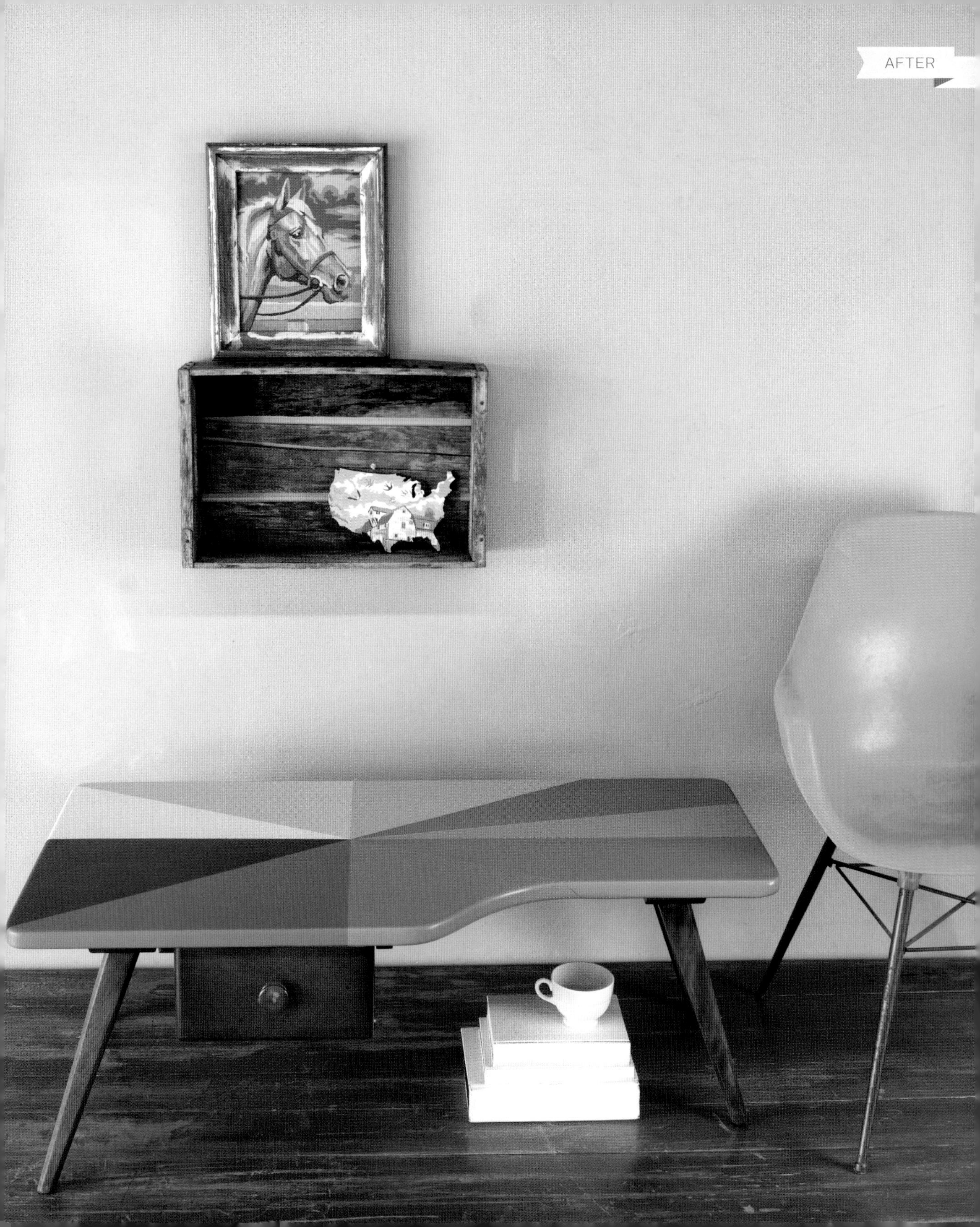

AFTER

MURIEL

This piece was purchased as a set along with the matching dresser (see page 166) at my local Salvation Army. I love the legs on this piece, and other than a few scratches and water marks on the top, it was in perfect condition. It's so fun and refreshing to find a piece that doesn't need any repairs and is ready to be painted immediately.

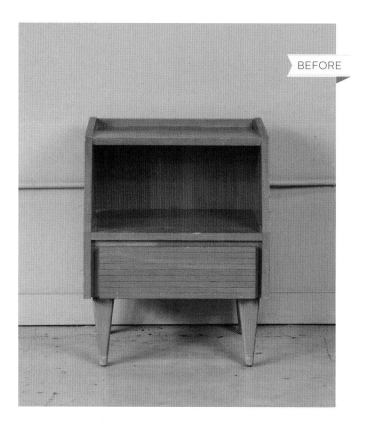

BEFORE

1 ▸ Refreshed the wooden legs with Danish oil

2 ▸ Applied handmade paper to drawer with Mod Podge (see Using Décou- page, page 88)

3 ▸ Applied polyurethane finish over the paper (see Applying Polyurethane, page 48)

4 ▸ Applied Minwax Special Walnut stain finish over the latex paint (see Stain- ing over Paint, page 56)

FREDERICA

I am a sucker for these little "pie-crust" side tables. They are called pie crust tables because the elevated, curved, and pinched edges look exactly like a homemade pie crust! The fluted legs, scalloped top, and triple pedestal base mean lots of room for creativity. You can really make these unique details stand out with paint, so I am always on the lookout for these types of pieces, and can find them pretty regularly.

BEFORE

1 ▸ Applied chalkboard paint on the top with a foam roller for an ultra-smooth writing surface (see Painting Furniture, page 52)

2 ▸ Applied Milk Paint with a Nylox brush (see Applying Milk Paint, page 72)

3 ▸ Lightly sanded with a fine sanding sponge to distress and remove loose paint

4 ▸ Added clear wax finish on the base only! (Do not put any type of finish on top of the chalkboard paint, or you will lose your chalkboard!) (see Waxing over Paint, page 58)

don't be like the rest of them, darling!

JULES

A friend who often stops by my studio gave me this lovely little treasure one day. At first I cringed at the beach theme and didn't think I would ever do anything with it. I hate to throw anything away, though, so I kept it on a shelf. After a while, I got an idea of what I could do with it and now it is one of my favorite pieces! For small pieces like this, I like to add an interesting detail in order to make it really special and unique. Patterned papers are the perfect material for this.

BEFORE

1 ▸ Applied paper accents with Mod Podge (see Using Découpage, page 88). I love this paper because of the colorful floral pattern and sweet birdie faces. This particular paper is a wrapping paper sheet purchased at Paper Source.

2 ▸ Applied latex paint with small craft brushes (small brushes work best for smaller pieces like this box). Lightly sanded with a fine sanding sponge for smoothing

3 ▸ Applied polyurethane finish over the entire piece (see Applying Polyurethane, page 48)

THE LOST BOYS

I found this collection of tables and stools while out hunting one day, and since I am a huge fan of collections and groupings, I just went for it and purchased them all. The condition was not horrible on any of these; they were just not appealing to me in their current state. I decided that a little mustard, grass green, light blue, and hot pink were in order.

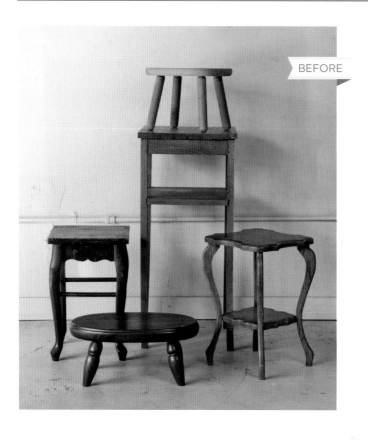

BEFORE

1 ▸ Taped off a design on top of the little green table (see Adding Stripes, page 96)

2 ▸ Spray painted each individual table in a beautiful bright color (see Spray Painting, page 112)

3 ▸ Added a clear spray coat finish (see Spray Painting, page 112)

MILK MEN

Glass bottles are everywhere, and I love to display them with fresh flowers, both in their natural state and painted. Bottles painted with a flat white paint take on a ceramic look that is beautiful and clean looking. Sprucing up bottles is a good way to give new life to something ordinary, and they make beautiful accents in any space.

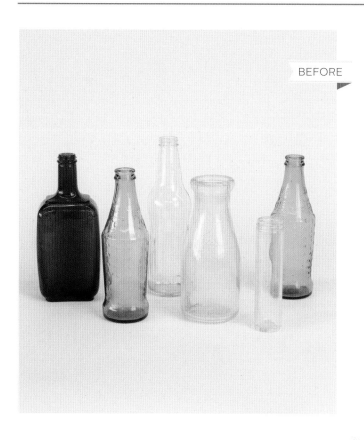

BEFORE

1 ▸ Cleaned out the bottles with warm soapy water and dried them thoroughly

2 ▸ Applied matte white spray paint in even coats, making sure to avoid drips (see Spray Painting, page 112)

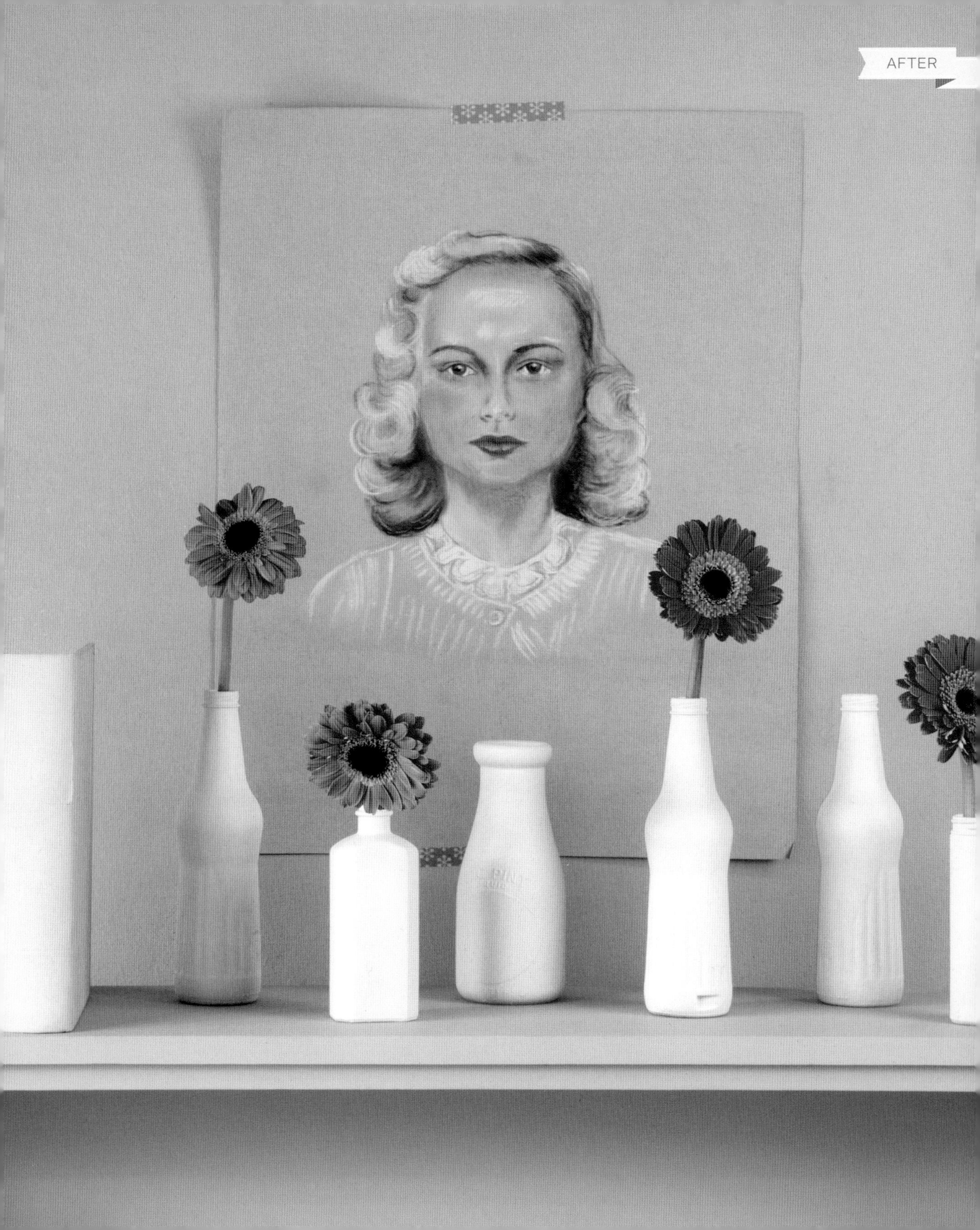

AFTER

ARTEMIS

This little oak chest is a custom job that I did for a client (who also happens to be a good friend of mine). This was an existing piece in her home that needed some updating and personality to freshen up the space around it. We put our heads together and came up with a design plan inspired by some pillows that she already had in the space, and I got to work. The pillows were traditional in color, with lots of tan, gray, mustard, and red and the fabric pattern was a beautiful modern block print. Using existing pillows and fabrics from the space for inspiration is a great way to create a cohesive design plan.

BEFORE

1 ▸ Removed the existing base, added a new base custom-built by a local craftsman, and added casters purchased from Home Depot

2 ▸ Left one drawer in the existing finish for a grounding effect; sometimes I like to leave some of the original piece in a design for authenticity.

3 ▸ Sanded and distressed the whole piece with a fine sanding sponge

4 ▸ Applied latex and stain (see Painting Furniture, page 52, and Staining over Paint, page 56)

BLANCHE

I purchased this piece off the back of a truck based on a photograph that was sent to me by the dealer! Oh my goodness it was such a mess, but I was determined to take it on. Bookshelves, believe it or not, are really hard to come by, so I knew I had to snatch this up. The original finish on this piece was a thick glaze that appeared to be smeared all over and then had finger paint designs on top of that! Yuck!

BEFORE

1 ▸ An hour and a half of sanding with an orbital sander to remove the texture of the glaze and smooth the entire surface (see Sanding Furniture, page 36)

2 ▸ Vacuumed the surface to remove all the dust and wiped it down with a clean rag

3 ▸ Applied latex paint with a foam roller for smoothness (see Painting Furniture, page 52)

4 ▸ Applied a water-based polyurethane finish (see Applying Polyurethane, page 48)

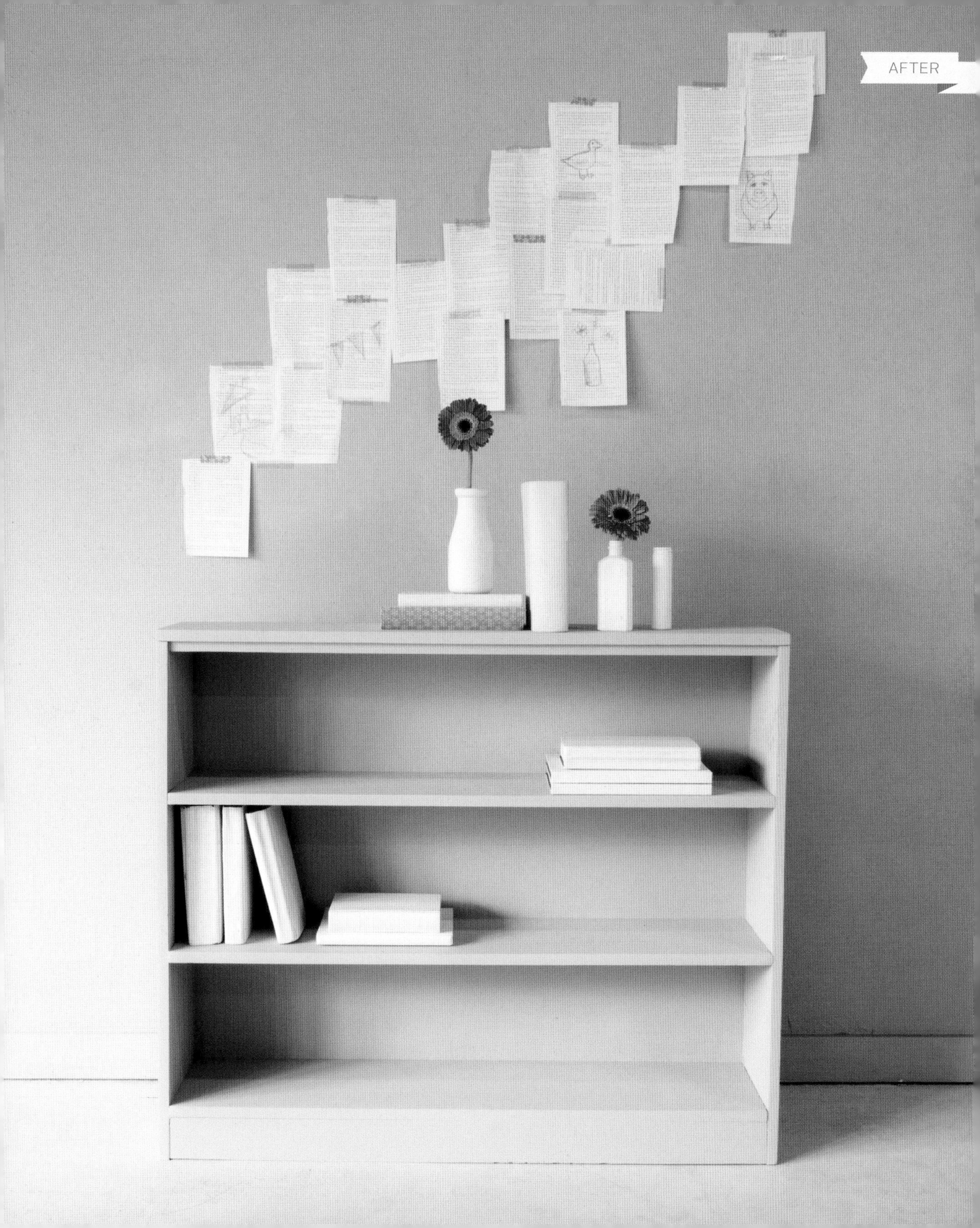
AFTER

LETTERS

My friend Lily spotted carts of bright yellow and red letters at a department store a little while ago. They were being thrown away during a store remodel. Knowing that I would love them, she loaded them all up and brought them to the studio. At first all I could think of was ketchup and mustard, but a little paper application did the trick. If you don't happen to come across a cart full of yellow and red letters (ha!), you can purchase wooden or cardboard letters at your local craft store.

BEFORE

1 ▸ Set the letters on the paper over a cutting mat and used a rotary blade to trace around them

2 ▸ Applied handmade paper with Mod Podge (see Using Découpage, page 88)

3 ▸ Sanded them lightly with a fine sanding sponge to remove any paper lingering on the edges

4 ▸ Applied a polyurethane finish (see Applying Polyurethane, page 48)

PETALIA

This sturdy little farm table was in great shape when I found it at a local antique shop. The flat top and curvy legs are right up my alley. I knew this table would be perfect for putting a design on the top because it had a nice wide, flat surface. A table like this is perfect for a breakfast area or casual family dining room. This piece would also make a great desk!

BEFORE

1 ▸ Traced a bike design (see Using an Overhead Projector, page 84)

2 ▸ Lightly sanded it with a sanding sponge

3 ▸ Applied the bike design in a gray latex satin-finish paint

4 ▸ Applied a polyurethane finish for protection and durability (see Applying Polyurethane, page 48)

LEE & CABOT

These two pieces were originally part of a desk, but had been removed into two separate pieces when I spotted them at a local antique shop. They had the wounds to prove it, and needed a lot of TLC. The sides of both pieces had to be repaired where they had been detached from the body of the desk. This was not a structural issue, rather a few holes and grooves that needed wood filling and sanding. I loved their perfect square shapes with very flat angles; they immediately invited a découpage finish.

BEFORE

1 ▸ Filled holes and seams with wood filler (see Wood Filling, page 40)

2 ▸ Cut paper in small to medium pieces and applied them to the entire piece with Mod Podge (see Using Découpage, page 88)

3 ▸ Applied a polyurethane finish (see Applying Polyurethane, page 48)

4 ▸ Added wooden knobs—these reminded me of an old ship!

EUDORA

This piece is solid and chunky, with curvy legs and insets that just beg for detail work. The curvy lines yield themselves to feminine finishes. When I got the piece, there were children's stickers all over the inside of the cabinet that had to be removed using a razor blade, and the doors would not stay shut due to missing hardware, but I knew I could turn it into a masterpiece.

BEFORE

1 ▸ Applied latex paint with a foam roller all over the piece (see Painting Furniture, page 52)

2 ▸ Applied gold leaf in the insets and as a stripe on the top (see Applying Metal Leaf, page 68)

3 ▸ Applied a Minwax Special Walnut stain finish (see Staining over Paint, page 56)

4 ▸ Added glass knobs with painted gold detail. No new holes needed to be drilled on this particular piece.

SELMA

Oh my goodness the fabric on this one was horrifying, but how fantastic is the detail of the wood chair frame? I knew the fabric could be easily replaced and saw potential for this piece immediately. This chair is solid and durable. With a little freshening up, it turned into something timeless.

BEFORE

1 ▸ Applied turquoise latex paint with a Nylox brush (see Painting Furniture, page 52)

2 ▸ Applied a brown wax finish (see Waxing over Paint, page 58)

3 ▸ Painted the upholstery tacks. I did not like the tacks in their original brass finish and wanted them to be a little more subtle on the fabric, so I painted them turquoise to match the wood finish.

4 ▸ Reupholstered the chair in a beautiful cotton woven fabric from Tony's Fabric

SHERMAN

One day I received a picture text from a friend saying that she was getting rid of this piece, and I decided to go take a look at it in person. I had to look past all of the gaudy brass hardware in order to see that this was a solid, heavy piece of furniture that could be long lasting. I have a hard time turning down rejected furniture pieces. It is like I am their last hope, and I am determined to turn them into something beautiful.

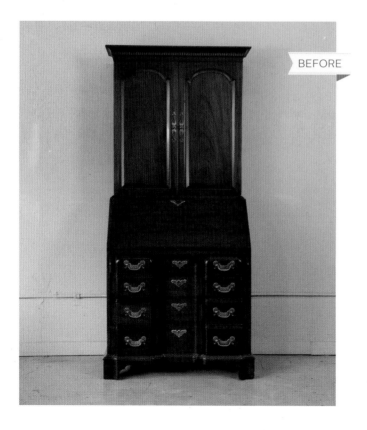

BEFORE

1 ▸ Removed all the hardware and filled holes on the sides where handles existed (see Wood Filling, page 40)

2 ▸ Taped off and spray painted the interior for an unexpected surprise when it is opened (see Spray Painting, page 112). I believe in going the extra mile to create exciting and interesting detail in my work, and love seeing people's faces when they open this piece and are greeted with a beautiful burst of color!

3 ▸ Taped off stripes on the side and front (see Adding Stripes, page 96)

4 ▸ Added new rope knobs purchased at Hobby Lobby

AFTER

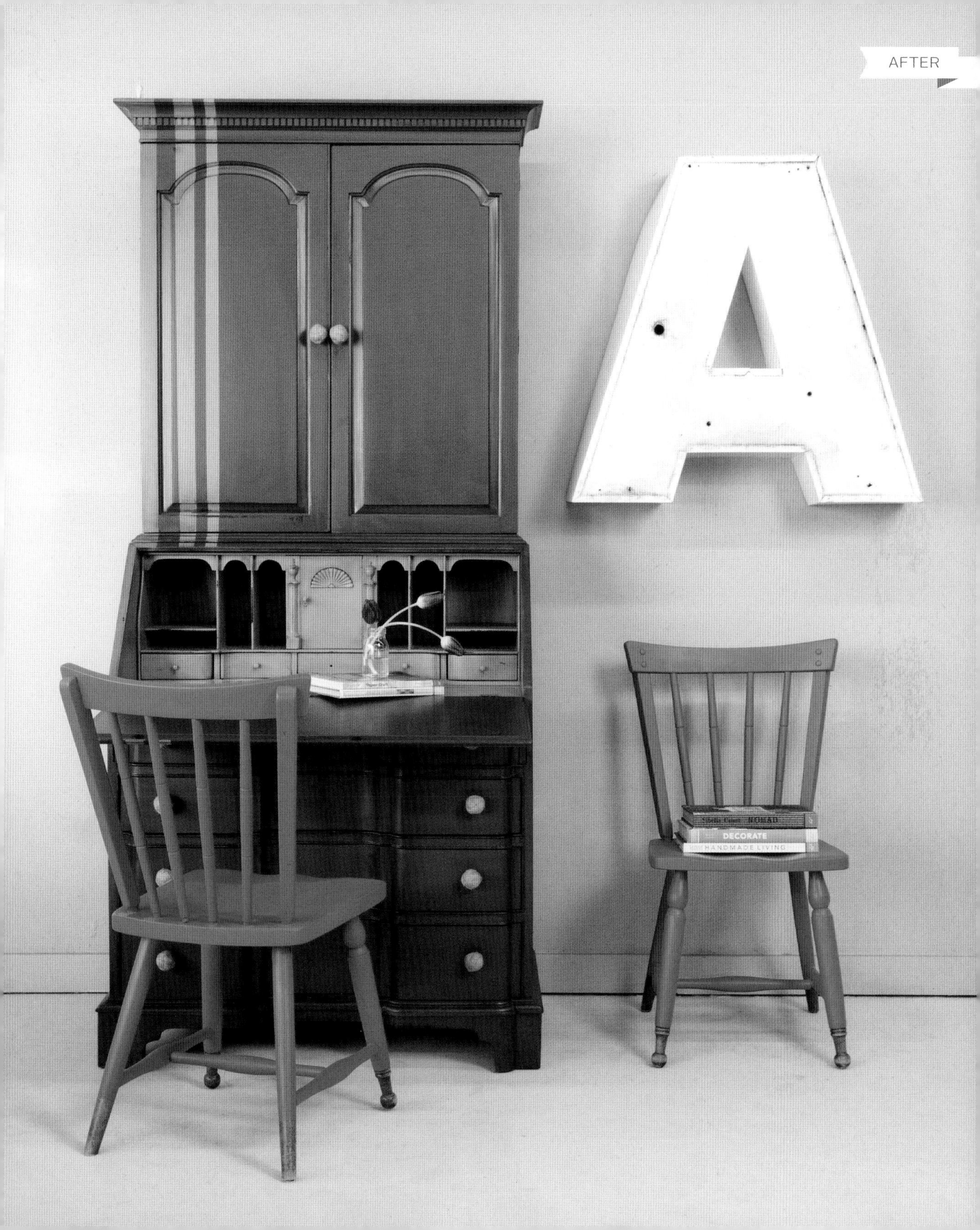

FLORA

I was drawn to this chair immediately because it had a great shape. I love the little spindle across the back, and the curved arms. I could just see it in a corner somewhere holding a stack of books, or around an eclectic dining room table.

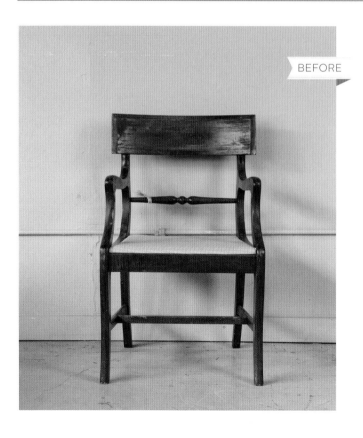

BEFORE

1 ▸ Upholstered the seat in a gray and white cotton ikat design (see Basic Seat Upholstering, page 114)

2 ▸ Painted chair with latex paint

3 ▸ Highly distressed the finish by hand

4 ▸ Applied a clear wax finish (see Waxing over Paint, page 58)

MINERVA

The large round pedestal base of this table had me at "hello." The tabletop had seen better days and had lots of peeling and pitted varnish, but I knew that with some good sanding and a bit of hard work, it could be beautiful and useful again.

BEFORE

1 ▸ Sanded the entire surface until it was nice and smooth using an orbital sander with a fine sanding pad (see Sanding Furniture, page 36)

2 ▸ Painted it with the dry brush technique (see Dry Brushing, page 104)

3 ▸ Applied a clear wax finish (see Waxing over Paint, page 58)

4 ▸ Hand sanded detail. After applying all of the paint, I stood back, eyed the finish, and went back in to hand sand out some detail that I wanted to see in the finish. I feel like this step is often overlooked and is key to getting a truly authentic finish.

MATILDA

When I first laid eyes on this piece, it was in the corner of an antique shop, stacked on top of a few other pieces of furniture. Honestly, I thought it was rather plain and dull. However, I loved the clean modern lines and decided to take a chance on her. She was a total blank slate, which is always fun.

BEFORE

1 ▸ Applied white paint with a foam roller for smoothness (see Painting Furniture, page 52)

2 ▸ Didn't do any distressing because I wanted a clean, smooth, and modern design for this piece.

3 ▸ Applied paper on the drawer front using Mod Podge (see Using Découpage, page 88)

4 ▸ Applied a polyurethane finish for protection (see Applying Polyurethane, page 48)

5 ▸ Added a new knob

AMABEL

This piece was modern and beautiful already, save for a few scratches and water stains on the top. I noticed upon further inspection that the drawers were sticking and almost walked away because I didn't want to mess with sanding and waxing down all of the drawers. Then I wondered if the drawers had just been put back in wrong, which is very common in antique stores, so I decided to move them around and see if that helped. It worked like a charm, and I brought her home for a makeover.

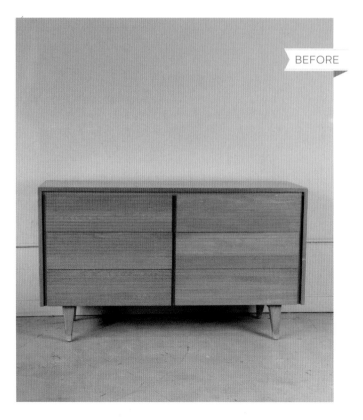

BEFORE

1 ▸ Used a reverse vinyl application to add a design (see Using Vinyl Decals, page 76)

2 ▸ Applied latex paint using a foam roller for a super smooth finish (see Painting Furniture, page 52)

3 ▸ Applied a polyurethane finish (see Applying Polyurethane, page 48)

4 ▸ Freshened the natural legs with Danish oil. (See Refreshing Wood with Danish Oil, page 62)

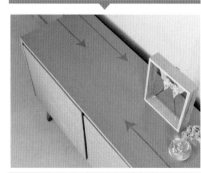

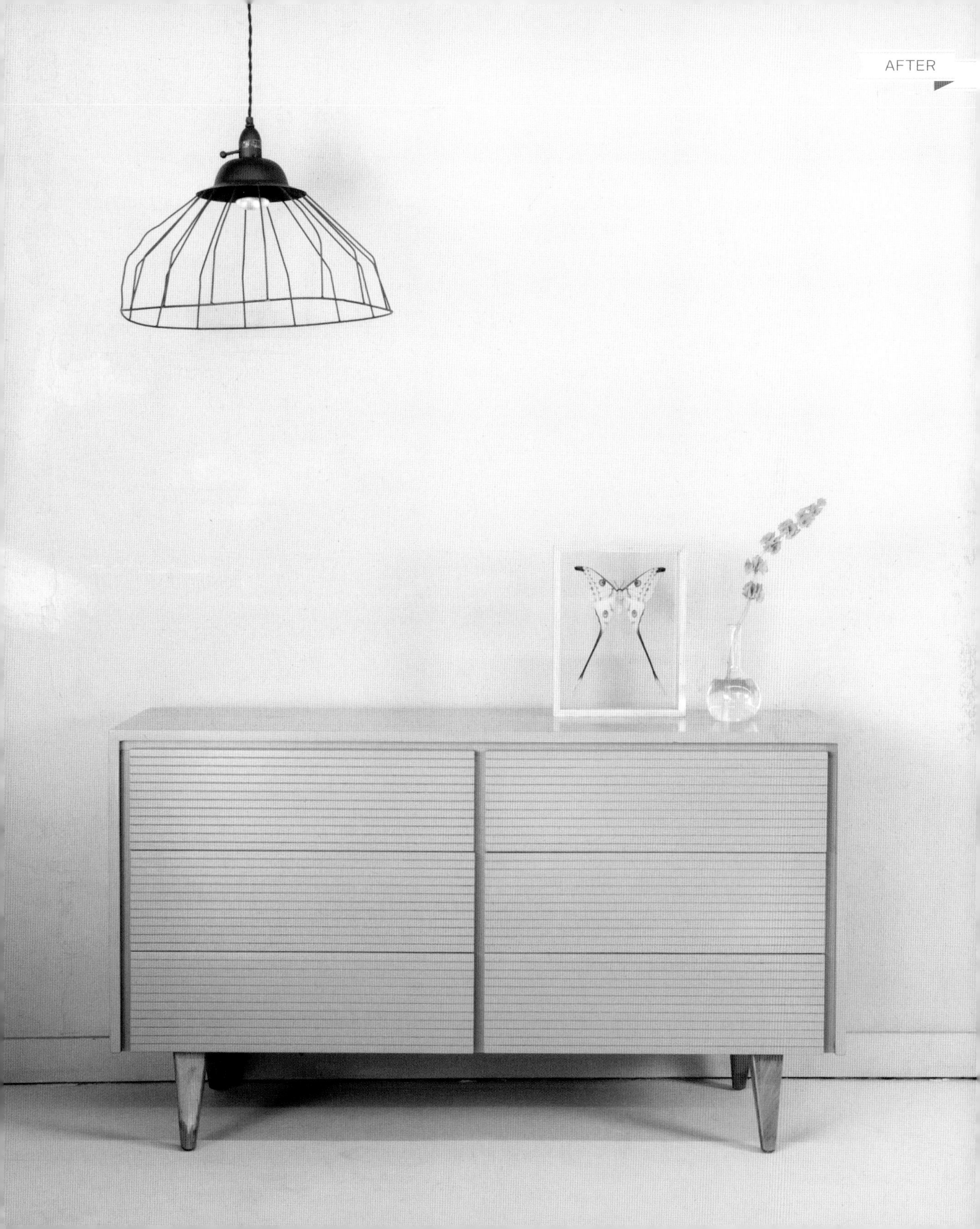
AFTER

COYETTE

I love any kind of old plank farm table. They are rustic, well built, and fit into many different design plans. The long turned legs on this one caught my attention for the specific purpose of dip-dying them.

BEFORE

1 ▸ Stripped the varnish off the legs (see Stripping Furniture, page 32)

2 ▸ Dip-dyed the legs (see Achieving the Dip-Dyed Look, page 100)

3 ▸ Hand sanded a distressed look

4 ▸ Applied polyurethane finish for protection (see Applying Polyurethane, page 48)

EMMALINE

My dad brought me this piece from upstate New York. It was at a garage sale, but the lady gave it to him for free because it was falling apart. When it arrived at my studio, it was literally tied together to keep it from falling into pieces. The repairs on this one were more than I could handle, so I did what I could by removing any and all loose wood, screws, and nails, and then took it to my friend Trey, who specializes in heavy repair work. All the work was worth it in the end. There are a couple of reasons I decided this piece was worth all of the repair and work, but the number one reason was that it was *free*, so I could afford to invest some money in heavy repairs. Items like this are extremely gorgeous statement pieces.

BEFORE

1 ▸ Removed all the nails and random wood pieces that had been applied crudely to this piece

2 ▸ Sanded it completely with an orbital sander on the flat surfaces, and a fine sanding sponge on the detailed wood carving and grooves (see Sanding Furniture, page 36)

3 ▸ Applied latex paint with a brush and foam roller (see Painting Furniture, page 52)

4 ▸ Applied a stain finish (see Staining over Paint, page 56)

5 ▸ Added gigantic glass knobs from Anthropologie

FAUSTA

This was another piece that literally showed up at my doorstep. The lady that brought it to me loved it, but had no use for it anymore and it did not fit her aesthetic. I was more than happy to adopt it because she is just so stunning. The piece has beautiful legs, and I have never seen drawers cut like these top drawers before. This before picture is a little deceiving because it looks like it is in great shape. What you can't see is that the whole piece wiggled back and forth when you touched it! I took this one to my buddy Trey for structural repair, and then started on my design plan. Whenever a piece has to be completely reworked (more than just a few glue and clamp areas), I like to take it to a skilled carpenter so that I can stand behind my work with 100 percent confidence in the repairs.

BEFORE

1 ▸ All joints taken apart and reglued (see Gluing and Clamping, page 43)

2 ▸ Applied milk paint (see Applying Milk Paint, page 72)

3 ▸ Applied an oil-based polyurethane finish (see Applying Polyurethane, page 48)

4 ▸ Dip-dyed the original hardware (see Achieving the Dip-Dyed Look, page 100)

THATCHER

This is a piece that I had custom built for the specific purpose of using a wallpaper application on it. I designed the entire piece so that I could apply wallpaper to the drawer fronts and side insets. Sometimes it can be hard to find the perfect piece for wallpapering, so I thought it would be fun to create my own piece to finish instead of having to go out and find that perfect piece. I commissioned a very talented local carpenter to build this piece for me. While having a piece custom built is definitely more expensive than using a found piece of furniture, it is another option in taking a blank furniture canvas and turning it into something spectacular with paint and paper. I really love how the design turned out—especially those little feet!

BEFORE

1 ▸ Applied latex paint to the whole piece with a foam roller (see Painting Furniture, page 52)

2 ▸ Applied wallpaper to the drawer fronts and side insets (see Using Découpage, page 88)

3 ▸ Lightly distressed the paint with a fine sanding sponge

4 ▸ Applied a polyurethane finish (see Applying Polyurethane, page 48)

PERPETUA

I purchased this piece at an estate sale, and it is by far the hardest piece I have ever worked on! A lot of the wood veneer was separated from the base and large chunks of veneer were missing on one side. It took several days of gluing, clamping, veneer removal, and sanding to get this piece ready for paint. It was totally worth it, though. This is a very unusual piece in design, and I have not come across another piece like it since. This is exactly what I look for in the statement pieces that I create, and the price on this one was bottom dollar, which gave me the incentive to put the hours and hours of work and repair into it. Uniqueness is key.

BEFORE

1. ▸ Glued, clamped, removed veneer, and sanded (see Gluing and Clamping, page 43, and Sanding Furniture, page 36)

2. ▸ Layered paint in two colors (see Layering Paint, page 108)

3. ▸ Applied a wax finish (see Waxing over Paint, page 58)

4. ▸ Spray painted the interior section (I removed the section to spray paint. I allowed to dry and then re-attached it to the piece.) (see Spray Painting, page 112)

5. ▸ Added little metal rose knobs for sweetness

me in pleasant places;
indeed, I have a
beautiful inheritance"

TULLIA

When I saw the routered panels on this piece, I knew it would be perfect for a paper detail application because the raised design with a grooved edge makes applying and trimming the paper application really easy. It is a built-in edge for the craft knife to slide along for a nice precise cut. I love the chunkiness of this piece, and the way the turned posts give it a bit of a soft look. A dark wood finish like this is one of my favorites to paint over with a black paint. When you add the brown stain over the black paint, it just looks so rich, warm, and beautiful.

BEFORE

1 ▸ Applied latex paint with a foam roller (see Painting Furniture, page 52)

2 ▸ Applied wallpaper in the insets (see Using Découpage, page 88)

3 ▸ Made detailed paper cutting with a craft knife

4 ▸ Applied Minwax Special Walnut stain finish (see Staining over Paint, page 56)

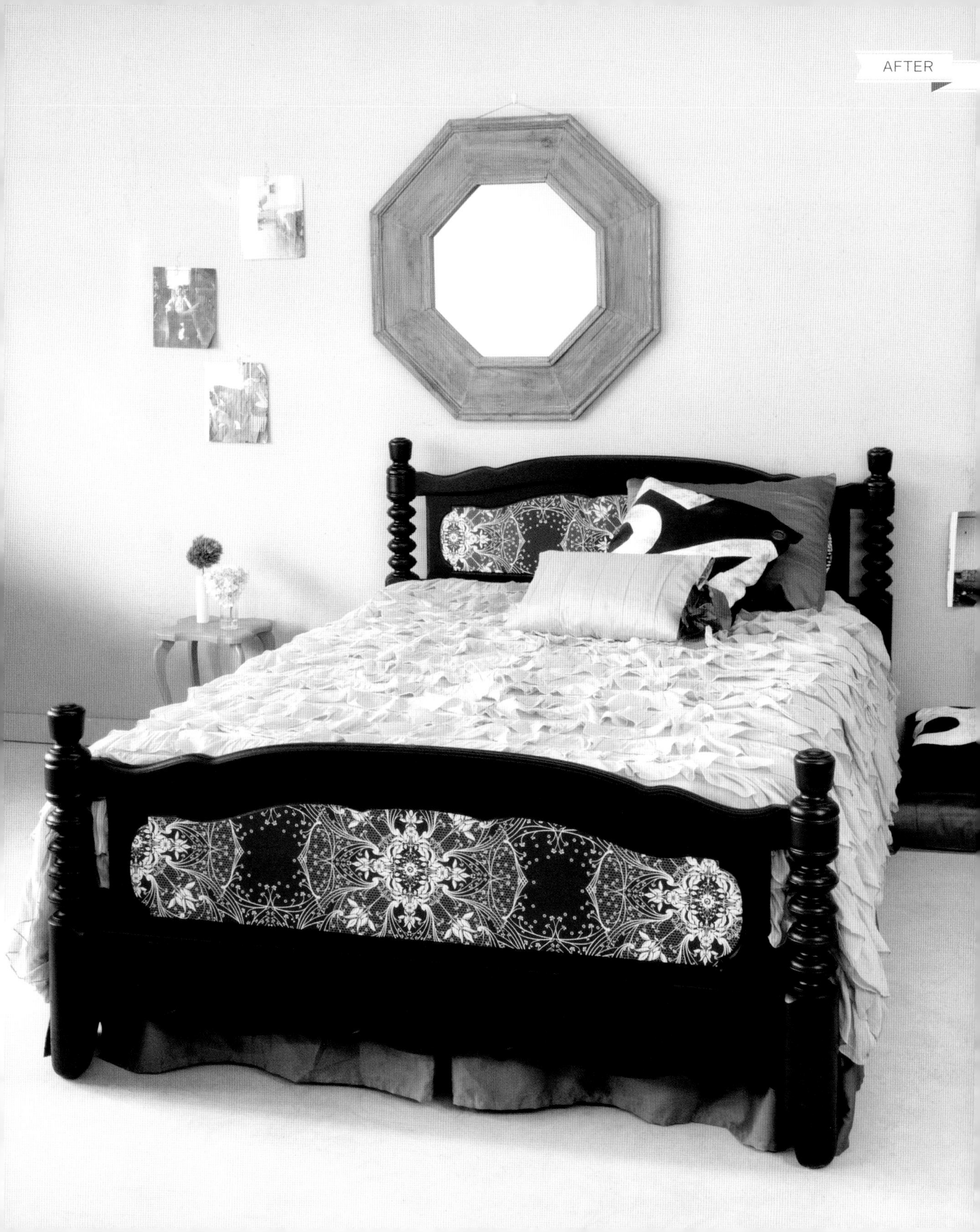
AFTER

ZELINA

Desks are very popular in my line of work, so I pick them up whenever I see them. I especially love this particular style of desk, with the beautiful feminine lines and the flower details. I am always, always drawn to detail on furniture because it just screams for paint. I could not wait to get some paint on those sweet little carved flowers!

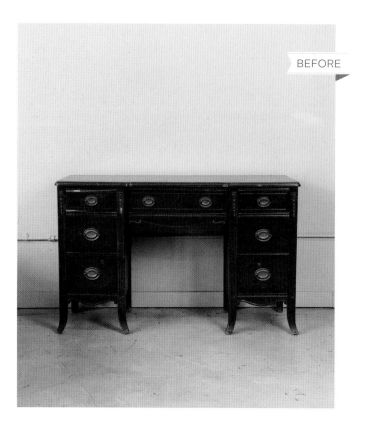

BEFORE

1. Designed a circle pattern with stencils (see Using Stencils, page 80)

2. Sanded over the paint for a washed and faded look

3. Stained over the paint with Minwax Special Walnut stain (see Staining over Paint, page 56)

4. Added pink ceramic melon knobs from Anthropologie

RESOURCES

In this section, you will find a list of my favorite resources for furniture finds, supplies, home decor, original art, and handmade goods.

FURNITURE FINDS

ANTIQUES ON AUGUSTA

This place owns a piece of my heart, as they have sold and supported my furniture for years. I have never seen a better curated antique store that is chock full of eclectic, traditional, modern, and rustic finds for the home. If you are in the Greenville, SC, area it is a place you will want to visit, and shipping is available for all out-of-town purchases.
6 S. Lewis Plaza,
Greenville, SC 29605
(864) 370-1870

GOODWILL

Goodwill Industries is always a great source for furniture, glassware, and unique vintage finds for the home.
www.goodwill.org

GREYSTONE ANTIQUES

My friend Trey owns this antique shop in Greenville, SC. Several of the pieces in this book were repaired by Trey and purchased directly from his shop. I buy in bulk from him, as he always has an abundance of what I am looking for. The really good news is that he ships out of state.
www.greystoneantiques.net

MIRACLE HILL MINISTRIES THRIFT

This is a great place to find quality furniture, although they are the highest priced thrift store in my area. I also tend to find really great glassware and unique vintage finds in this store.
www.miraclehill.org

SALVATION ARMY

The Salvation Army is the thrift store where I seem to find the most (and best!) furniture pieces, and their prices are hard to beat!
www.salvationarmyusa.org

FLOWERS

AMY OSABA

Amy designs the most beautiful flower arrangements. On pages 2, 75, 155, 171, 173, and 183 you will find her amazing work, and I am honored that she drove all the way from Atlanta one day to do flowers for this book. Truly the stuff dreams are made of. *www.amyosaba.com*

FRESH MARKET

Fresh market always has a beautiful assortment of fresh flowers. *www.thefreshmarket.com*

TRADER JOE'S

Trader Joe's is another source for florals, potted herbs, and of course dark chocolate peanut butter cups for "energy" while painting (wink!). *www.traderjoes.com*

WHOLE FOODS MARKET

Whole Foods is my absolute go-to location for fresh and reasonably priced florals. Fresh flowers are like bread and butter for me, and I love to use them for multiple weekly photo shoots in the studio and in my home. I can always run out, even last minute, and find a great assortment in the Whole Foods floral department. *www.wholefoodsmarket.com*

TOOLS & MATERIALS

ACE HARDWARE

Ace Hardware is my source for casters and Krylon spray paint. They have the best prices on spray paint, and keep all of my favorite colors—both new and old—in stock. *www.acehardware.com*

ANTHROPOLOGIE

Anthropologie is just a great place to find hardware treasures. While most people may be headed in to look at the amazing clothes and displays, I make a beeline for the hardware and knobs section! I also find great wallpapers here. Find a store near you or order online. *www.anthropologie.com*

BENJAMIN MOORE

Benjamin Moore paints are near and dear to my heart, especially the Aura paint line. The colors available are just fantastic, and the paint is smooth, creamy, and never thick. This is my first-choice paint for use in all of my furniture makeovers. *www.benjaminmoore.com*

COST PLUS WORLD MARKET

World Market recently started carrying hardware and knobs, but the main reason I pop into this store is for all of the gorgeous handmade paper. *www.worldmarket.com*

ETSY

Etsy is a great online source for fabric, prints, unique handmade items, home accessories, and vinyl designs. The vinyl arrows used in the technique on page 76 were purchased through an Etsy shop: www.etsy.com/shop/WallumsWallDecals *www.etsy.com*

HOBBY LOBBY

The national chain Hobby Lobby is another great source for knobs and hardware, and they are always 50 percent off, so you can find great hardware at really great prices. *www.hobbylobby.com*

HOME DEPOT

This is my playground, and I can get lost looking at all of the tools, supplies, and gadgets that catch the eye of a gal like me. This store is one-stop shopping for all of your furniture makeover needs. *www.homedepot.com*

JENNY LEIGH DESIGN

Jenny Leigh Design is where I purchased the Chalk Paint used in the layering paint technique on page 108, and also where you can purchase the wax brush that I love so much. This wax brush is a must-have tool! *www.jennieleighdesign.com*

JU JU PAPERS

This is a small hand-printed wall-paper studio in Portland, OR. All of the wallpapers are screen printed by hand and are made to order. I used some of Avery's gorgeous wallpaper in the technique on page 64.
www.jujupapers.com

LOWE'S

Another playground of mine. Also one-stop shopping for tools and painting supplies.
www.lowes.com

MICHAELS

I think the Michaels stores have such a beautiful selection of crafting supplies, and I tend to get lost on the aisle with all of the Martha Stewart glitters, papers, and tools. The wood-grained paper used as a background on pages 135 and 165 was purchased from Michaels.
www.michaels.com

OLD-FASHIONED MILK PAINT

Milk paint is my favorite paint to work with, and the most authentic in finish. If you do not have a local store that carries milk paint, here is the place to get it!
www.milkpaint.com

PAPAYA

This is a great online source for wrapping paper and other very colorful and artful home décor pieces.
www.papayaart.com

RALPH LAUREN

I really love the creamy consistency of Ralph Lauren paint and have several go-to colors in this line. I usually purchase all of my Ralph Lauren paint locally through Suburban Paint Co., but if you do not have a local retailer that carries Ralph Lauren paint, you can look up the closest retailer to you or order it online.
www.ralphlaurenhome.com

STENCIL 101 DECOR

This book by Ed Roth is full of stencils and is a great tool for adding art work to furniture. I heart it!
www.stencil1.com

SUBURBAN PAINT

This is my favorite art supply and paint store in Greenville, where I purchase Benjamin Moore paints and all of the Montana Gold spray paint that I use in my spray painting projects. It is a family-run business with a super friendly, experienced, and talented staff. I am always blown away by the over-the-top customer service that makes this a favorite stop of mine.
www.suburbanpaintco.com

TOUCH OF EUROPE

This is another great online resource for beautiful paper products, and where I purchased the clipper ship paper used in the découpage technique on page 88.
www.touchofeurope.net

WOODCRAFT

I am known at my local Wood-craft store as the "milk paint girl"! I specifically buy all of my milk paint in this store. What I love about Woodcraft stores (available nationally) is that all of the employees are skilled woodworkers and have a vast knowledge of paints, finishes, and different types of wood.
www.woodcraft.com

HOME ACCESSORIES

IKEA

IKEA is one of my favorite sources for fabric, paper napkins, organizational pieces, lighting, and home accessories. I love the Swedish influence and simplicity in design that is abundant in this store.
www.ikea.com

POTTERY BARN

Pottery Barn is a great source for linens, lighting, and rugs.
www.potterybarn.com

TARGET

Target is a wonderful place to shop for just about anything, but I love that they pair up with fantastic designer labels to create not only affordable, but great design for the masses. Target carries a beautiful selection of home goods and accessories.
www.target.com

THOMAS PAUL

I love everything that Thomas Paul creates for the home, especially the pillows and melamine dishware. The colors and graphics in his designs are just gorgeous.
www.shopthomaspaul.com

ARTISTS & UNIQUE FINDS

ART AND LIGHT GALLERY

Mid-century lighting, furniture, and artwork are abundant in this fusion gallery. It has an impressive selection of modern home accessories.
www.artandlightgallery.com

CARRIER STUDIO

The founder of this studio, Angie, is a fantastic collage artist, fabric designer, and painter. You can see her fabulous butterfly pillows on page 127 and her butterfly chair on pages 8 and 177.
www.acarrierstudio.com

CRANNY

A super-great Etsy shop run by my sister, Cranny is chock-full of fabulous yarn wreaths, yarn trees, photography, fabric garlands, and so much more. The yarn wreath on page 125 is from Cranny's shop.
www.etsy.com/shop/ crannyfoundfavorites

DIANE KILGORE CONDON

She is a Greenville artist and friend who creates stunning artwork that really just has to be experienced to be believed. The bird paintings on page 125 are by Diane.
www.artbombstudio.com

JOSEPH BRADLEY STUDIO

Joey's use of color is amazing and the softness of his painting is simply beautiful. The owl painting on page 155 and the deer painting on page 171 are just a couple examples of his fantastic work.
www.josephbradleystudio.com

KEEP CALM GALLERY

This gallery is a really great online source for any kind of print, especially letterpress. The framed alphabet print used on page 169 was purchased here.
www.keepcalmgallery.com

KOELLE ART

Annie Koelle creates gorgeous paintings of birds, bugs, landscapes, and geographic prints. One of the reasons I am so drawn to Annie's work is her use of found frames and objects to create the backdrop for her light and airy work. The hawk painting on page 173 is a personal favorite.
www.anniekoelle.com/ home.html

LILY WIKOFF

Lily is a very talented ceramic artist and creates the most beautiful ceramic vessels, jewelry, and succulent gardens.
www.lilywikoff.com

ROYAL BUFFET

My paper moose head has created quite a name for himself, and has kind of become a trademark for Knack Studio. All of the paper garlands and papier mâché animal heads used on pages 127 and 175 were made by my friend Mollie Greene of Royal Buffet.
www.molliegreene.com

SOMETHING'S HIDING IN HERE

I have always been a fan of this talented husband and wife team, and admire their keen eye for design and resourceful artwork. The paint-by-number cutout of the United States on page 133 is a favorite purchase of mine!
www.somethingshidinginhere .com

INDEX

ACKNOWLEDGMENTS

I am indebted to my Creator for all He has bestowed upon me, for His example to me of seeing the lovely in the unlovely, and for His creations in nature that inspire my work on a daily basis.

To my amazing husband and best friend, Jon, whose love gave me wings and taught me to breathe. Your support of my passions and dreams, your enthusiasm for my work, your love for our family, your ever-present smile and laughter, and your all-around awesomeness make me the luckiest girl in the world! Thank you for your patience during this project and for not only holding down the fort, but for making our fort the most peaceful and well-run fort around. The laundry, cleaning, dishes, meals . . . you handled it all, and "thank you" just does not seem like enough. I love you forever.

To my children, Conley and Brynn, I am so thankful for the two of you, and you guys are the greatest blessings I have ever received. Conley, your tender heart, quick wit, silly one-liners, and crazy techno music make me smile. Brynn, you wake up singing, you have a magical personality, you come up with the best color combinations in your outfits, and your love of people and animals is just beautiful. I love you guys to the moon and back.

To my parents, I love you. Thank you for instilling in me a love of travel, garage sales, color, and for teaching me the value of hard work and using the resources that you are given. I am so thankful for the heritage that I have in our family. Dave, Mark, and Sarah, I love you all and am thankful to have such supportive and loving siblings. Thank you for encouraging and cheering me on the whole way!

To my pal Lily, I will always remember that moment in 2007 when you took a giant leap with me and split a little 600-square-foot studio! Both of us were scared to death, and didn't know if we would be able to pay the rent, but we did it together and I will never forget.

Dreams became reality on that day and it has been so fantastic to watch all of those dreams and goals we talked about for both of our businesses come to fruition. Thank you for taking many hours out of your busy schedule to help with the planning and photo shoots on this project. You are a gem.

To Aaron, thank you for the many hours you spent photographing this project with me, for your amazing organizational skills, and for putting up with all of my craziness. You are fantastic at what you do, and I was lucky to have you on my team.

To all of my pals who stepped in and painted, cleaned, built photo displays, brought coffee, sat on my dirty, sanding dust–covered studio floor and hung out, helped me shop, sent me emails and encouraging messages, and were there for me this entire project . . . *thank you*! I am so blessed to be surrounded and loved by you all.

Special thanks to Marian McCreight Designs for the use of picture frames, metal chairs, vintage chandeliers, and any other styling aid I could get my hands on. Special thanks to Dale Peters of Alana's Upholstery for always creating fabric masterpieces and for actually showing me how to "spit nails."

To my editor, Laura Lee Mattingly, thank you for believing in my work and this project. I am so thankful for the countless hours you spent working on this dream of a project, and how you helped me turn it into a reality. I could not have done it without you. It was truly, truly a pleasure to work with you.

To my agent, Stefanie Von Borstel, you are the smartest smarty-pants girl I know! You made all of the overwhelming technical details of this project a piece of cake, and I never had to worry about any of it. That is huge, my friend. Thank you!